The Assassination

of a

Mind

ISBN 978-0-9858029-0-5

The

Assassination

of a

MIND

Folkston, Georgia a small Southeastern town with the population of 2502.

Not too much is heard of this town, at least until now. You will be surprise as to what goes on behind their little door.

This door is opening and what you will see and hear is unbelievable.

I was behind this door and inside is nothing good. It brings memories of the 30s, 40s and 50s.

To get caught behind this door you will be assassinated and probably buried alive.

Tune in to this true story and let your mind be assassinated.

This is a true story

II

The Assassination of a Mind

Inside Look

The Assassination of a Mind is written to prove the boundary line from a sound mind to insanity. Most of us have crossed this line many times in our lives. Understanding when you reach this point helps minimize the feelings generated by the conflict.

When these conflicts take place other forces falls into play. The characteristics of his family present themselves accurately. The strongest gene whether it male or female roles out the carpet.

This book will show good loving men and women process this ugly element that you would not believe. To you this is not the truth but I will assure you this book is the truth. If you meet anyone of these people and they say this book is fiction; you tell them they are lying.

Contents

The Beginning

Joseph (Joe) Jordan an African American male was borne August 14, 1896 in Charlton County, GA.

His Father was named Laze Jordan.

I have no record of his early childhood. This story starts in August, 1944.

Joseph (Joe) Jordan was a laborer in the Timber Industry. He had nine children. (That I found records of) They are Phyllis Jordan, Rosella W. Grace, Vernell Williams, Lillie Mae Harvey, Robert Jordan, Alberta Myers, Joseph Jordan, Samuel (Sammy) Jordan and Mary Lou Jordan.

His wife was named Elizabeth Maynor. Elizabeth was borne September 28, 1900 in Baldwin, Florida. Her father was Steve Maynor.

At the age of forty-eight (48) Joe Jordan made a great contribution to his family. On August 01, 1944 he purchase sixteen (16) of land from J. W. Buchanan.

This land was located about two miles west of

 town on Gibson Post Road of Old Paxton Place better known Route 152

.

Raising his children and taking care of his family was a great appetite that

Joe Jordan enjoyed.

The Family enjoyed this land about fifteen (7) years without any major problems.

October 10, 1951 Joe Jordan issued a Warranty Deed to Albirtha Turner. The measurements for this land are 110'x130' which is 0.50 acre.

OF GEORGIA, CHARLTON COUNTY.
THIS INDENTURE, Made this 10th day of Oct. in the year of our Lord One Thousand Nine Hun-
and Fifty-One between JOE JORDAN of the State of Georgia and County of Charlton of the
part and ALBIRTHA TURNER of the State of Georgia and County of Charlton of the second

WITNESSETH: That the said party of the first part, for and in consideration of the sum
rty and No/100 ($30.00) DOLLARS in hand paid at and before the sealing and delivery of
presents, the receipt whereof is hereby acknowledged has granted, bargained, sold and
ed and by these presents does grant, bargain, sell and convey unto the said party of the
part, her heirs and assigns, all that tract or parcel of land lying and being in the
istrict, G. M. of Charlton County, Georgia, and particularly described as follows:
ing at the Southeast corner of tract owned by Eliga Hannan, and running from said Point
Easterly direction along the North side of Public Road leading to the Gibson Community,
ince of One Hundred and thirty (130) feet to a stake, thence in a Northerly direction a
e of 110 feet to a stake, thence west a distance of 130 feet to a stake corner, and thence
utherly direction a distance of 110 feet back to the place or point of beginning. Said
being bounded as follows: On the North and East by other lands of Joe Jordan, the
herein, on the South by Public Road leading to Gibson Community, and on the West by
f Eliga Hannan.
HAVE AND TO HOLD the said bargained premises, together with all and singular the rights,
and appurtenances thereof, to the same being, belonging or in any wise appertaining, to
y proper use, benefit and behoof of Her the said party of the second part, her heirs
igns, forever, IN FEE SIMPLE.
d the said party of the first part, for Himself, His heirs, executors and administrators
rant and forever defend the right and title to the above described property unto the
ty of the second part, her heirs and assigns, against the lawful claims of all persons
er.
WITNESS WHEREOF, The said party of the first part has hereunto set his hand and affix-
eal, the day and year above written.
                                              JOE JORDAN   (Seal)

sealed and delivered in the presence of
Jones
cQueen, N.P.
al affixed)
 April 15, 1952
W. REYNOLDS, CLERK
* * * * * * * * * * * ** ** * * * * * *

After years of marriage Joe and his wife began to have

problems so he divorced her.

He wanted to keep the family in a close surrounding
therefore he provided her shelter.

On April 03, 1961 Joe Jordan deeded Elizabeth an acre of
land. This acre of land was a 210 ft square.

WARRANTY DEED—FORM 17

Foote & Davies, Inc., Atlanta, Ga.

STATE OF GEORGIA CHARLTON County.

THIS INDENTURE, Made this 3rd day of April in the year of our Lord One Thousand, Nine Hundred and Sixty-one , between

JOE JORDAN

of the County of Charlton and State of Georgia of the first part, and

ELIZABETH JORDAN

of the County of Charlton and State of Georgia , of the second part.

WITNESSETH, That the said part y of the first part, for and in consideration of the sum of Two Hundred and no/100 ($200.00) – – – – – – – – – – – – – – – – – DOLLARS in hand paid at and before the sealing and delivery of these presents, the receipt whereof is hereby acknowledged, as granted, bargained, sold, and conveyed, and by these presents do es grant, bargain, sell and convey unto the said part y of the second part, her heirs and assigns, all that tract or parcel of land lying and being in Charlton County, Georgia, to wit:

ALL that certain lot, tract or parcel of land situate, lying and being in the 32nd G.M. District of Charlton County, Georgia, containing one (1) acre, more or less, having the following metes and bounds:

BEGINNING at the point on the lane leading from the Gibson Post Road to the Old Joe Jordan House, said point being on the westerly edge of said lane, and also being the northeasterly corner of lands owned by Alberta Farlow, thence running westwardly along the northerly land line of lands of Alberta Farlow a distance of 210 feet to a point (said point being the northwesterly corner of lands of said Alberta Farlow); thence running northwardly in a straight line parallel to the westerly right-of-way line of the aforesaid lane leading from the Gibson Post Road to the Old Joe Jordan House a distance of 210 feet to a point; thence running eastwardly in a straight line parallel to the aforesaid northerly land line of lands of Alberta Farlow a distance of 210 feet to a point on the westerly right-of-way line of the aforementioned lane; thence running southwardly along the said westerly right-of-way line of said lane a distance of 210 feet back to the place or point of beginning.

Said lot or parcel of land hereby conveyed is in the shape of a square, each side being 210 feet in length, and is bounded as follows: Northwardly and Westwardly by lands of Joe Jordan; Eastwardly by the aforementioned lane leading from the Gibson Post Road to the Old Joe Jordan House (said lane being the property of Joe Jordan); and Southwardly by lands of Alberta Farlow.

Said lot or parcel above described is a part and portion of that certain tract of land conveyed to Joe Jordan by J. W. Buchanan's Executor in deed dated August 1, 1944, recorded in the public land records of Charlton County, Georgia, in Deed Book "2", page 82; specific reference being hereby made to said deed and the record thereof for description and all other legal purposes.

He had a house built for her by Jim Walter Corp; P. O. Box 9128, Tampa 4, Fla

This was a shell house four rooms built without an inside bathroom. Later he added an extension on the back of the house for a bathroom. The house had only four (4) rooms in the beginning.

One year later Joe Jordan also gave Willie V and Lillie Mae Harvey (daughter) an acre of land on April 24, 1962. This acre was located in front of the Elizabeth Jordan home

Another year later on June 19, 1963 he gave his son (Robert Jordan) a deed for only a half of an acre (0.50). This 0.50 acre is located on the Westside of Willie and Lillie Mae Harvey. The land was given to Jim Walter Corp for a shell house.

There address was Jim Walter Corp, P. O. Box 9128, Tampa, Florida.

There were problems but not serious to warrant special treatment.

After many years passed some say Elizabeth mind was getting inactive. She had a case of Arteriosclerosis Heart disease.

Around April in 1972 she had to be admitted to Central States hospital in Milledgeville, GA.

Elizabeth died August 04, 1972 of acute heart failure at the Central State hospital in Milledgeville, GA.

She stayed there three (3) months and Twenty-seven (27) days.

On the death certificate Joe Jordan listed her as married. In a sense he was thinking that was still his wife. Therefore everything she owned became his property. No family member had or made any arguments as to what belongs to whom.

7

After the death of Elizabeth, Joe Jordan moved into the house he built for her. The house was above ten years old.

As the years go by we find out that the seeds from Elizabeth Jordan are embedded in a few of her children.

Some of the children grew up and moved away to other cities to continue their lives.

Years later Joe Jordan got sick and not any of the family living around him would give him care. (I know of Alberta Myers a daughter and Robert Jordan a son).

Lillie Mae Harvey (daughter) who was living in Punta Gorda, Florida with her family heard the bad news. The love she had for her father got her immediate attention to move back to Folkston, Georgia.

She packed up her family and came to Folkston to take care of her father.

Lillie Mae and family made their home in Folkston, Georgia. Their children attended the local schools. In between caring for her father Lillie Mae was able to hold down small jobs.

9

Attending to her father and working was a burden and many days her father seen the results. Within his mind I know he had thoughts of thankfulness and was very grateful.

Ownership of Land Transferred

On March 17, 1976 Joe Jordan did the ultimate thing. He realized Lillie Mae was the only child that took care of him. On this date he made Lillie Mae the only Heir to all his land.

He made the deed for seventeen (17) acres instead of the sixteen (16) acres he purchase. The extra acre was the acre he deeded to his wife Elizabeth. When he dies he wanted to make sure his daughter Lillie Mae got everything.

STATE OF GEORGIA   CHARLTON   COUNTY.

THIS INDENTURE, Made this 17 day of March in the year of our Lord One Thousand, Nine Hundred and (76) Seventybetween Six

JOE JORDAN
of the County of CHARLTON and State of GEORGIA , of the first part, and LILLIE MAE JORDAN HARVEY

of the County of CHARLTON and State of GEORGIA , of the second part, WITNESSETH, That the said part y of the first part, for and in consideration of the sum of TEN DOLLARS AND OTHER VALUABLE CONSIDERATION++++++++++++Dollars, in hand paid at and before the sealing and delivery of these presents, the receipt whereof is hereby acknowledged, ha s granted, bargained, sold, and conveyed, and by these presents do grant, bargain, sell and convey unto the said part y of the second part, heirs and assigns, all that tract or parcel of land lying and being in

the 32nd Dist. G. M. of Charlton County, containing seventeen acres (17) more or less, bounded on the South by Gibson Post Road, West by Bud Altman Road, North by lands now owned by Norris Johnson and East by Hatcher Branch.

This land is the same deeded 9 June 1945 from C.S. Buchanan as executor of the Estate of J.W. Buchanan. in Deed Book 2, page 83 and 84 in the office of Clerk of Superior Court Charlton County Georgia.

LIFE ESTATE
The grantor herein reserves a life estate in and to the above described property for and during his natural life.

CHARLTON County, Georgia

Real Estate Transfer Tax

Paid $ -0-

Date 3-7-78

Lois B. Mays
Clerk of Superior Court

TO HAVE AND TO HOLD the said bargained premises, together with all and singular the rights, members and appurtenances thereof, to the same being belonging, or in anywise appertaining, to the only proper use, benefit, and behoof of LILLIE MAE JORDAN HARVEY the said party of the second part, heirs and assigns, forever, in fee simple.
And the said party of the first part, for his heirs, executors, and administrators, will warrant and forever defend the right and title of the above described property unto the said part y of the second part. heirs and assigns, against the claims of all persons whomsoever.
IN WITNESS WHEREOF, the said party of the first part ha s hereu hand and affix ed his seal , the day and year first above writte Signed, sealed and delivered in the presence of

11

Let me give you the information I learned about the last paragraph. Joe Jordan purchase sixteen acres and he made a will (deed) to Lillie Mae Harvey for seventeen acres. The other acre was his wife Elizabeth. Therefore Lillie Mae had a will that was recorded for seventeen acres.

Let me also put my thoughts into what was going on.

Joe Jordan purchases sixteen (16) acres from J. W. Buchanan.

In 1951 he deeds Albirtha one-half (0.50) acre

In 1961 he deeds his wife one (1) acre.

In 1962 He deeds Lillie Mae one (1) acre

In 1963 He deeds Robert one half (0.50) acre

That is three (3) acres.

He only had 13 acres left

If you look at what he did in a business sense; you would think Lillie Mae Harvey and Robert Jordan owed him for their lands.

The records can be access from Jim Walter and we all might be surprised as to why he did this.

I am willing to bet the above is the way it went.

Let's look at the law: If the estate does not have any property to pass on in the will (because property passed automatically to a co-owner or spouse) a probate is not necessary, though it still needs to be filed in Probate Court. If this is the case, there's no cost for filing the will.

Lillie Mae Harvey had a will and the will was for seventeen acres. No family Member asks to have any of this land probated.

You have to ask yourself: "Why would Probate accept a will and some twenty years later deny it exists?" One Attorney told me "The Courts wants specifics; a deed is not a will but if Charlton County been doing business this way; that the way things are done and have to be accepted by law".

This is the way Charlton County done business.

Around November 1976 Joe Jordan needed care around the clock. He was placed in Folkston Nursing Home. He lived there around three (3) months.

January 17, 1977 Joe Jordan died at the age of eighty (80) years old. That was a sad day for Lillie Mae but she knew she done the best she could taking care of her father.

Lillie Mae had no money therefore; she offered to divide the land among her family if they help bury their daddy. No one hope and this really brought sadness to Lillie Mae. The family was angry because their daddy gave all the land to Lillie Mae. No mention of probating Elizabeth Jordan acre.

Lillie Mae had to think fast and her only option was to mortgage the land.

She redrew lines and made it possible to single and adds as needed for the Mortgage Companies.

She Mortgage a portion of the acre in Elizabeth Jordan name. Strange thing this was in 1978 to 1980 and no one mention about Probating Elizabeth Jordan acre. Even the mortgage companies accepted the records from the court house.

14

An Ugly Marriage

Lillie Mae had a daughter name Rose Marie. I met Rose in 1994 while driving for Greyhound in Jacksonville, Florida.

We met a few times when she said she was married to Kenneth Reed. All her kids are his except the oldest. (Jarvis) I asked was she divorced from the children father. She said yes. I told her I was divorced also.

After I learned that her Father was a Deacon and Mother was a solid church member, I was very pleased. We decided to start dating.

Rose came to my apartment in Jacksonville and most times I would prepare dinner for her and the kids. The kids seem to be happy about our relationship.

I started going to her house in Folkston, GA. I notice from time to time the children's father would come around. Everyone seems to get nervous or afraid whenever this happen. I was not because if she is divorced I have the authority to be there.

I met with my old friend (Joe) who lives in Jacksonville and told him the news. I am getting married and moving to Folkston, GA. He begged me not to move to Folkston.

He said I should know how small towns work. He was borne in one like me and I should know. I smile and told him I was in love and this is my last chance at a loving life.

When I left he seems very unhappy with my moving. I really am thankful to have a friend to really care for me.

In January 1995 Rose got very ugly. I am not sure if she was seeing someone or wanted out of the relationship.

I wrote her this letter and today I do not know why I continue with this relationship.

Dear Rose,

Today is a sad day in my life. I've
had to make things work for us. I'm
one always being hurt.

I make a silent promise to myself this
morning. I also come back inside before leaving
let you know the results. Never the less they
do matter to you.

Well let me explain something to you.
When I made a promise to continue my will
to make you happy. This is true
I'll accept anything less then the same
in my partner.

I were serious about the picture
that picture when it was first taken I
told you I liked it very much. You said
it wasn't right for me to have it yet you
got a naked picture of you lay around
were everyone can see it. There is no

17

Georgia Department of Human Resources

VITAL RECORDS UNIT

STATE FILE NO. _____

COUNTY NO. _____

Marriage License

STATE OF GEORGIA   COUNTY OF _____Charlton_____

To any Judge, Magistrate, Minister of the Gospel, or any other person authorized
to solemnize: You are hereby authorized and permitted to join in the Holy State of Matrimony

Ralph Leon Watts (B-58) *and* Rose Marie Harvey (B-36)

according to The Constitution and Laws of this State, and for doing so this shall be your sufficient
license.

Given Under My Hand and Seal, this ²⁴ᵗʰ day of _____March_____ 19 95

_____
Probate Judge

I hereby Certify, That _____Ralph Leon Watts_____ *and*

Rose Marie Harvey _____ were joined together in the Holy State

of Matrimony on this ²⁵ᵗʰ day of _____March_____ 19 95 by me in the

City of _____Folkston_____, County of _____Charlton_____, Georgia.

Recorded _____3/27/95_____ 19____

Signature of Official _____Elder John Wesley Scott_____

Book No. _____4"H"_____ Page _____652_____

Title _____Minister_____

Rose and I got married March 25, 1995. All the family members
seem happy to accept me into this family.

18

I put most of my things in storage at Folkston and moved into her house. I did notice some of the children father clothes were still in the house.

Everything went well for the first couple of days.

Then I got a phone call that someone had broken into my storage unit. My computer and valuable things were taken. I had no insurance on these items. This really hurt because I had valuable information on my computer.

I didn't realize this was a sign for me to leave Folkston.

About the fifth day the children's father came to the house. He was drunk, cursing and acting as if being tormented with calamities.

The next day I went to the Sheriff office. I told him everything that went on the day before. I asked him to please send a deputy around to this man house. Let the deputy tell him not to come back.

A few days later this happen again. This time I got Rose's father (Willie V. Harvey) to go with me to the sheriff office.

The Sheriff asked: where's the wife?

Immediately I went to Rose and asked her to get a restraining order to keep this from happening. She refused with the idea he was the children's father and he had a right to be here too. Then at this very moment I knew this was not the place for me.

I drove for Greyhound Lines and most of my trips I would have to stay overnight. When this happen I would call home late at night and Rose would not be home.

When I return and question why is she out late and not home with the children. Her response was "Mama is next door and she would see after the kids".

Things began to make sense to me. These impressions I were receiving facilitated my faculty of perception. I was beginning to understand good judgment and moral character was missing from this family.

To document this saying: I came home after work and the children were watching television. I noticed they were watching an X-rated movie. Rose baby daughter (3 year old) was seated in front of the television. I asked them not to watch movies of this nature. They replied you're old fashion and we do this all the times.

When Rose came home I express my feeling to her and she agreed with the kids. She told me I were old fashion and besides these are her kids. If she wants the kids to watch these movies; they watch them. What a way to raise children.

Here I felt a barrel of rejection. The next day I went into the local grocery store. When I came out the store an older man approached me. After we introduced ourselves he began to tell me the background of the Jordan/Harvey family.

Unbelievable things I was told but three things stood out. The first: Rose was not divorced from the children's father. The second: Robert Jordan is a troublemaker, jealous and wants to boss people around. Third: Rose had a family member who set the house on fire and sat in a corner of the house and burned herself up. Now I really got afraid of what I was involved in.

Again I came home and asked Rose about her divorce. She said she was never married to Kenneth and she didn't need a divorce.

Now I knew for sure I must get out of this house. I really didn't want anything to do with bigamy. (Bigamy is a felon). This woman does not care anything about the law. The state of Georgia accepts and recognizes common-law marriages.

Common law unions legal in Georgia

Dear Call Box: A bunch of us seniors go to Burger King every morning and argue about whether there is a common law marriage in Georgia. Could you settle this? — **B.C., Brunswick**

Dear B.C. A marriage without a license and ceremony is called "common law," according to the Fulton County (Ga.) Superior Court Family Division. Such marriages are recognized in various forms in about 15 states and the District of Columbia. Florida is not one of them.

If the common law marriage was established in Georgia before Jan. 1, 1997 or was legally established in a state that still recognizes common law marriages, then it is a legal marriage in Georgia.

While restrictions vary, a typical common law marriage requires more than living together; the couple must present itself as husband and wife.

"In most states that recognize common law marriages, there are no time requirements for living together," the Superior Court said on its Web site (www.fultonfamilydivision.com). "The controlling issue is not time together, but the intentions of the parties."

Also, to help people learn more about the legal system, we found a Web site with many tutorials: www.nolo.com.

Dear Call Box: Will the Skyway be available for trips for an event downtown that starts at

Peter Je

By Tim Cuprisin
Milwaukee Journal Sentinel

They are two of the men who Sept. 11 with all of us.

And, in so doing, ABC's Peter nings and CNN's Aaron Brown formed a function that has be part of our culture, a role that Cronkite created nearly four d ago, the day John F. Kennedy

"The great, lasting image of kite is that he takes off his gla us that the president has died great, black, horn-rimmed gl wipes away a tear," Brown sa he did we all cry. He venting television at that mo

Jennings and Brown are in fraternity of anchors who co inventing TV news last Septe They spoke last week in sepa phone interviews.

"It was one of those days o you thank your lucky stars fc been given the opportunity some experience," recalled who has anchored ABC's eve

CLB	B	AT	Broadcast		7:00	F
			3 NBC	NBC News 421237		(C
3	3	3	4 IND	Entertainment Tonight (CC) 7701		In (C
25	25	25	5 PBS	The NewsHour W Lehrer: Top storie		
8	8	8	7 PBS	The NewsHour W Lehrer: Jim Lehre journalists detail th stories. (CC) 4352		
			8 PBS	Hidden Worlds: River; otters. (CC)		
			11 CBS	CBS News 429904		9 (L
11	11	11	12 NBC	Wheel of Fortune (CC) 7985		J K
9	9	9	17 WB	Friends: Reconciliation. (CC) 76850		J E d h
			20 ABC	9/11: Reporters cc		
			22	9/11: Reporters cc		

When you read this you will see Rose is still married to the children father.

She lived with him for many years and they had three children together. She had some accounts in his name Rose Reed. Now she is still married to her children father and will not recognize the law. You have got to accept what the law says.

She married again to some guy in Jacksonville, Florida and still living the life of a bigamist which is a felon. She has to be very careful because Jacksonville Police are very efficient. Most people comes to Duval county be investigated. If they find out she is a felon (bigamist) running free they will pick her up.

The husband can also be charged with the same crime. That is the reason I asked for an annulment. I could be charged if I marry a bigamist. I wish them luck and good fortune but I want to abide by rules of the right law.

She will not outtalk enforcement in Duval County like she does the enforcement here in Folkston, GA. Bigamy is a felon and most law enforcement agency do not let felons go free. But as long as she lives in Folkston she does not have to worry about that felon. Her friends at city hall will not arrest her. Good luck with that!

These things happening were really embarrassing to me. When you want and try to live a righteous life all the devilish things jump out at you. I thought about my children. They will think I have loss my mind to get involved in all these ugly activities.

Old Friends Hangout

In Jacksonville, FL I usually hang out at a Krystal on Lem Turner.

Most of these guys are Deacons, Preachers and good church members. They entertain and usually keep each other happy.

One old friend name Joe asked me "Why you seem so unhappy lately?" I gave a cheap smile and answered "Everything is OK"

They looked at me in a very unusual way. My looks must have told them something.

"OK I will tell you" Cleared my throat "My marriage did not work out and I might have problems with that family."

Joe said "Man we thought you had lost it, moving to Folkston is not good

 for Black Folks".

 I smiled and said "African Americans do not have a problem there".

 I cleared my throat. "It those kids wearing their pants hanging off their behinds".

 I continued. "Jacksonville is the same way, Kids walking around showing their stinking underwear."

 I went on "They will not work; they steal and make Senior Citizens very uncomfortable".

Joe said; "You are right, we have lost a generation".

 I got up "Let me tell you guys something; I really appreciate your thoughts and I think you all are great to be around". Points toward my car: "Me and Betsey must get in the woods-that is home you know"

"Take care yourself" Joe said. (Shaking his head in sorrow)

I left for Folkston, GA.

The weeks passed as I'm looking for a place to stay.

One day Rose's mother came and ask me to buy an acre of land. She shows me the acre and an old raggedy house that sits on it.

The next day I went down to the Court House and check the court records. The records show this property was clear. The clerks assured me the records are kept up to date.

One thing I must say: Folkston have the best Clerk of Superior Court in the world. Kay Carter and her employees hope and gave me information that was very informative. I am very grateful for their service, understanding and kindness.

[That statement was written for the 1990s. I happen to return to the Clerk of Superior Court office in 2012. It was not the same as stated in the earlier years. They weren't informative as before and less caring.

I think they were less active because of their workload and subjected I get an attorney. I know they did not know I was qualified to lookup cases. I bought and sold houses in Jacksonville, FL for many years. I had to do my own work looking up cases. It was computerized but the same system.

Also I remember all those letters I wrote to the Clerk of Circuit Court asking the Court for a continuance, help, etc. I wanted to exchange my attorney. I never received any answer to any of the letters. Those letters were address to Kay Carter who was the Clerk. Man! I was just in the dark about everything and was not treated well after all.]

The next day this was September 9, 1995. I agreed to buy that acre.

She said an acre is worth $2,000.00 but if you can do better I sure would appreciate it. She needed money in a bad way.

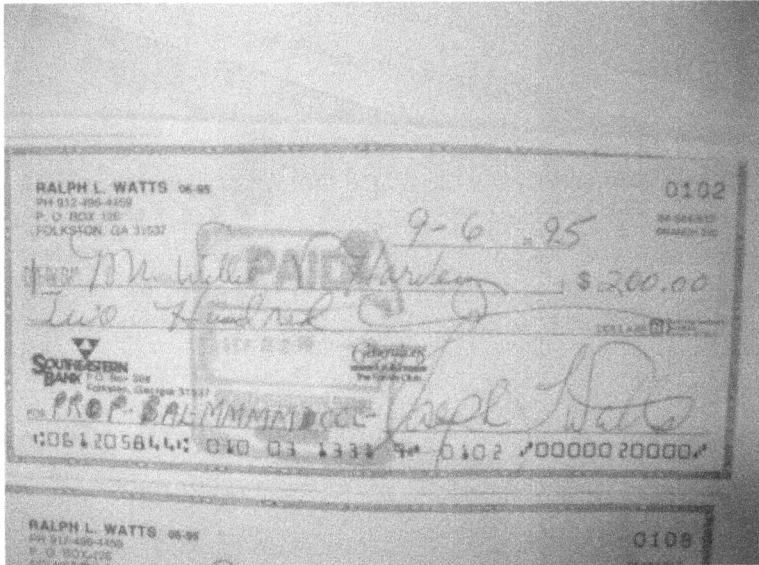

She had been a great Mother-in-law. She always was trying to get her daughter (Rose) to act better. Therefore I decided on my own to give the family $5,000.00 for the acre.

I made a check out to her husband with the balance noted on the check. Check #0102: Payment $200.00 with a balance of $4,800.00

I went over and check the old house that was still standing. This house wasn't good enough for a dog to live in. The front and back doors would not close. The windows were broken or rotted out. The house smells something terrible with many rooms of fire damage. I had no choice but to move in this house to get away from Rose.

I told Rose I had to leave; we cannot stay together. I would not live and make this a part of my life. Christ was in my life and to go out and party was not my type of living. I immediately moved in that old raggedy house of Elizabeth Jordan

Let me tell you I had to recall my thoughts. While I was thinking I realized how I got into trouble. I left God out of my decision makings. If I had prayed and ask for God's help he would have led me in the right direction.

Instead, I decided on my own what looked good was good for me. That is how the Devil got in and leaded me in the wrong direction. Man cannot do well by himself. He does not possess the power to withstand the Devil's duties.

In early 1996 I found a corner in one room in this old house where I could place a bed without being rained on. I placed a bed there and began to repair this old house. The other part of the room was pots and pans catching water when it rains. (it rained everyday).

When I moved in this house the neighbors laugh and booed at me. This was not a good feeling for me. Here I am with a good job and living like a hobo.

The house was without electricity. The well was broken and has to be repaired. Their son Bobo (Willie & Lillie Mae) who lived in the house caused it to catch on fire.

Bobo (nick name) had a water line running from his father's house across the road. This is the way he got water to the house when he was living there.

The house had to be repaired and inspected before I could get electricity. At this time it was very cold and the wind was plowing through all the cracks and holes,

I purchase a kerosene heater and used one room to live in. That was the only room that had a door where I could half close. Anyone could just walk right in to my bunk. I prayed and thank God for protecting me.

I would go to my job two hours early to take a bath and change my uniform before going to work. This went on the whole winter. Believe me this was very tough living.

On March 19, 1996 in Bibbs County (National Lending Center) Lillie Mae executed a deed for 12.52 acres. It had a division of four (4) Tracts. They are Tract #1=9.18 acres; Tract #2=1.76 acres; Tract #3=1.12 acres and Tract #4=0.46 acre. This makes a total of 12.52 acres. Tract two includes a portion of Elizabeth Jordan acre.

Still twenty years later no one said anything or question the mortgage company about probating Elizabeth Jordan's acre.

April 22, 1997 Lillie Mae and husband Willie made a deed to (me) Ralph Watts and Wife (their daughter) Rose Harvey. The deed was made for one acre of land. This acre of land was a portion of the original acre Joe Jordan deeded to his wife.

32

The old house was not mention because it was worthless. Most of the windows were broken out. It rains in all the rooms and little water was available from a line ran from Mr. Harvey's house.

Still nothing was said about probating Elizabeth Jordan acre.

On March 19, 1996 in Bibbs County (National Lending Center) Lillie Mae executed a deed for 12.52 acres. It had a division of four (4) Tracts. They are Tract #1=9.18 acres; Tract #2=1.76 acres; Tract #3=1.12 acres and Tract #4=0.46 acre. This makes a total of 12.52 acres. Tract two includes a portion of Elizabeth Jordan acre.

68/

——————————————————— [Space Above This Line For Recording Data] ———————————————————

Loan No. 9602298

SECURITY DEED

THIS SECURITY DEED ("Security Instrument") is given on **MARCH 19** , 19 **96**
The grantor is **WILLIE V. HARVEY AND LILLIE MAE HARVEY, HUSBAND AND WIFE**

("Borrower").

This Security Instrument is given to **NATIONAL LENDING CENTER, INC.**

which is organized and existing under the laws of **THE STATE OF GEORGIA** , and whose
address is **700 W HILLSBORO BLVD, B1 #204,**
DEERFIELD BEACH, FL 33441 ("Lender").
Borrower owes Lender the principal sum of
THIRTY THOUSAND AND 00/100

Dollars

(U.S. $ **30,000.00**). This debt is evidenced by Borrower's note dated the same date as this
Security Instrument ("Note"), which provides for monthly payments, with the full debt, if not paid earlier, due and payable
on **MARCH 25, 2011** . This Security Instrument secures to Lender: (a) the repayment of
the debt evidenced by the Note, with Interest, and all renewals, extensions and modifications of the Note; (b) the payment of all
other sums, with interest, advanced under paragraph 7 to protect the security of this Security Instrument; and (c) the performance
of Borrower's covenants and agreements under this Security Instrument and the Note. For this purpose, Borrower does hereby grant
and convey to Lender and Lender's successors and assigns, with power of sale, the following described property located in
CHARLTON County, Georgia:

SEE ATTACHED SCHEDULE "A".

Charlton County, Georgia
Georgia Intangible Tax Paid
$ 90.00
Date 03-29-96
Monroe Todd   com
Tax Commissioner

which has the address of   **RT 2, #1 & #2 GIBSON POST RD**   **FOLKSTON**
[Street]   [City]
Georgia   **31537**   ("Property Address");
[Zip Code]

TO HAVE AND TO HOLD this property unto Lender and Lender's successors and assigns, forever, together with all the
improvements now or hereafter erected on the property, and all easements, appurtenances, and fixtures now or hereafter a part of
the property. All replacements and additions shall also be covered by this Security Instrument. All of the foregoing is referred to
in this Security Instrument as the "Property".

BORROWER COVENANTS that Borrower is lawfully seised of the estate hereby conveyed and has the right to grant and convey
the Property and that the Property is unencumbered, except for encumbrances of record. Borrower warrants and will defend generally
the title to the Property against all claims and demands, subject to any encumbrances of record.

GEORGIA - Single Family - Fannie Mae/Freddie Mac UNIFORM INSTRUMENT
Form 3011 9/90
Laser Forms Inc. (800) 446-3555
LIFT #3011 5/93   Page 3 of 6
Initials: LMH WVH

34

Still twenty years later no one said anything or question the mortgage company about probating Elizabeth Jordan's acre.

April 22, 1997 Lillie Mae and husband Willie made a deed to (me) Ralph Watts and Wife (their daughter) Rose Harvey. The deed was made for one acre of land. This acre of land was a portion of the original acre Joe Jordan deeded to his wife.

The old house was not mention because it was worthless. Most of the windows were broken out. It rains in all the rooms and little water was available from a line ran from Mr. Harvey's house.

Still nothing was said about probating Elizabeth Jordan acre.

35

QUI

LILLIE-MA

RALPH AND ROS

GEORGIA,   C

CLERK'S OFF

Filed,   Apr

3:45

Deed
Book   44

Kay

SOUTHEASTERN BANK

DARIEN, GEORGIA 31305

PURCHASER   Ralph & Rose Bothe

NOTICE TO CUSTOMER
AN INDEMNITY BOND MUST
BE PURCHASED IF THIS
CHECK IS LOST OR STOLEN.

5/28/9

DATE   May 28, 1

PAY TO THE
ORDER OF   Lillie Mae Harvey $ 2,000.

SOUTHEASTERN 2000dh00cts

CASHIER'S CHECK   NON-NEGOT

36

May 29, 1997 I gave Rose a check for $1,000.00. This
was half of a loan. Check #0272

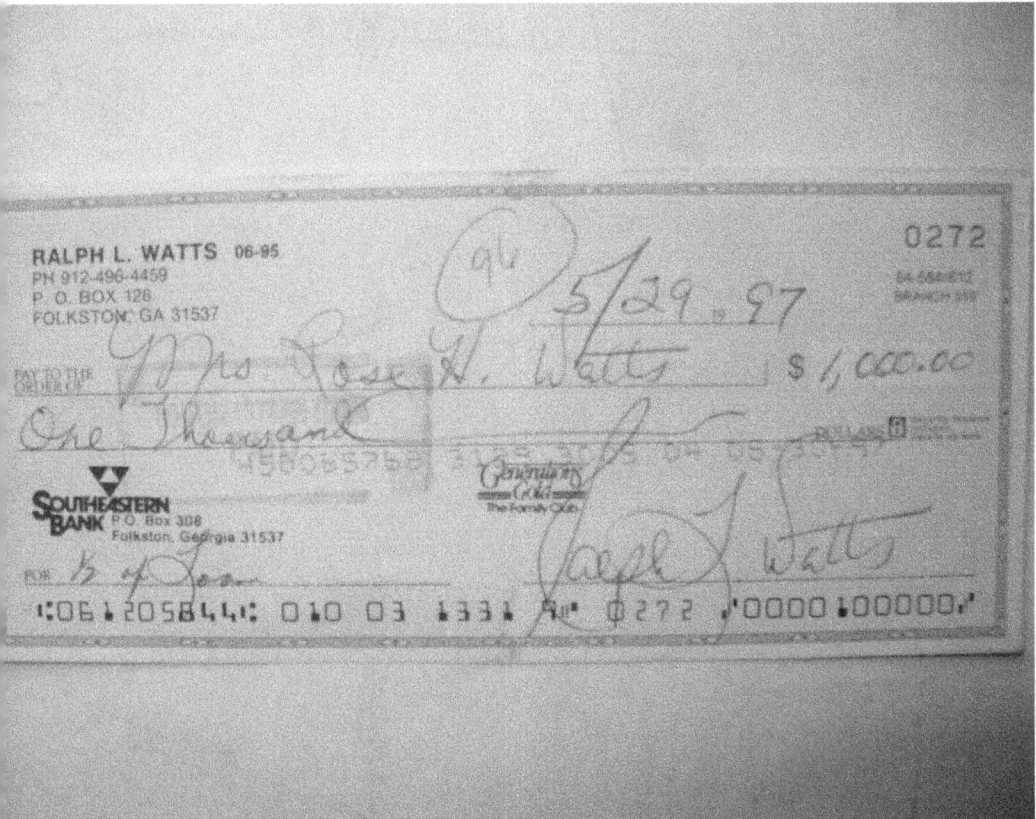

June 30, 1997 I applied for electric service at my house.

Okefenoke Rural Electric Membership Corporation

POST OFFICE BOX 602	2475 VILLAGE DRIVE	POST OFFICE BOX 1229
NAHUNTA, GA 31553-0602	SUITE 106	HILLIARD, FL 32046-1229
912-462-5131	KINGSLAND, GA 31548	904-845-7477
912-462-6100 FAX	912-882-1362	904-845-7510 FAX
800-262-5131		

These We Serve

Whom It May Concern:

ne: RALPH L. WATTS

ling Address: PO BOX 36, FOLKSTON, GA 31537

lectricity currently connected to this service address? Yes No

Watts applied for service at this location 6-30-97, service was put into Mr. Watts' ne as of 7-2-97.

mpleted by: Mandy

le: Customer Service

) If Lillie Mae Harvey is not allowed to change or make a deed, and then the original deed should stand.

Therefore the drawing should look like this:

The Plat below shows the acres in 2004. It does not show Elizabeth Jordan true acre. The true acre is a 210 square (dotted square). A large potion of the Elizabeth Jordan acre drawing below belongs to Lillie Mae Harvey. It was not in the original deed made by Joe Jordan.

Below is what Elizabeth Jordan acre is supposed to be. The dotted line is Elizabeth Jordan acre. (210x210

39

40

The dark area is Lillie Mae Harvey private property. A-B-C-D

The square area is Elizabeth Jordan acre. E-F-G-H

As you see Robert Jordan cannot give me a deed for Lillie Mae Harvey private property. He can only make a deed for Elizabeth Jordan acre which is a 210x210 square.

In August 1997 I learned Rose was trying to use my name for credit. Immediately I went to the local newspaper and had an article printed for everyone to know I will not be responsible for no bills other than my own. (This is documented)

42

March 06, 1999 Rose signed a Partnership Agreement:

This agreement was made up because she needed money. She asks me to get it from Southeastern Bank and she would keep up the payments.

Below is the signed agreement and Rose did not pay a penny. I was stuck with this bill.

43

PARTNERSHIP AGREEMENT

This is an agreement between Ralph L. Watts and Rose H. Watts.
Rose Watts agree to accept responsible for half of the mortage note made this day 03/06/1999.

REASONS BELOW

Rose Watts had an accident with her vehicle. There was no insurance on the vehicle. Therefore, Rose agreed to pay half of the note if I refinance the existing mortage.

The existing mortage was with Southeastern Bank. ACCOUNT # 071594. Balance on loan was 10 payments @ 186.93 each.

This agreement shall exist whether or not the marriage continue. If by some unfortunate reason one or the other defaults, this does not excuse him or her from their responsible.

If one party defaults, the defaulter shall be responsible for all attorneys and court costs.

The parties above and below signed and agreed to these terms. Any future developments shall not affect this agreement.

Ralph L Watts 3/6/99
RALPH L. WATTS

Rose H. Watts 3/6/99
ROSE H. WATTS

44

From time to time Rose would come and borrow money without paying me back. This was a going trend so I had to find a way to document what was going on.

Rose had an accident without insurance coverage. She came to me to sign a loan at Southeastern Bank to repair the two cars. I agreed only if she sign an agreement to the payback.

She agreed and signed the agreement. She never paid any on the agreement.

In November 1999 she wanted more money. I told her the only way I'll help her is to sign the Elizabeth Jordan acre over to me. At this time I had not done any work on this raggedy house. This house didn't look good and she didn't want it anyway.

On November 19, 1999 she signed the deed over to me. (This is documented) I gave her a satisfactory amount of money. I didn't worry about her signing for the money. I knew I was not going to get it back. I had her name off this deed and I can start repairing this old raggedy house.

STATE OF GEORGIA,   CHARLTON   County

THIS INDENTURE, made this 19th day of November In the year of our Lord Nineteen Hundred and Ninety-nine between Ralph Watts and Rose Watts of the County of Charlton of the first part and Ralph L. Watts of the County of Charlton of the second part:

WITNESSETH that the said parties of the first part, for and in consideration of the sum of TEN Dollars and other Considerations Dollars in hand paid, the receipt whereof is acknowledged, have bargained, sold and by these presents do remise, release and forever quitclaim to the said party of the second part Their heirs and assigns, all the right, title, interest, claim or demand the said parties of the first part has or may have had in and to

ALL That Tract or Parcel of Land situate, Lying and being in the 32nd G.M. District of Charlton County, Georgia, containing ONE (1) Acre, more or less, having The following Metes & Bounds
(See CORRECTION Deed filed January 19, 1999 In Deed Book 47, page 406)

CHARLTON COUNTY, GEORGIA
REAL ESTATE TRANSFER TAX
FILED JULY 14, 2000
AMOUNT $-0-
Kay Carter
CLERK OF SUPERIOR COURT

With all the rights, members and appurtenances to the said described premises in anywise appertaining or belonging.

To Have and Hold the said described premises unto the said party of the second part heirs and assigns, so that neither the said parties of the first part nor Their heirs, nor any other person or persons claiming under GRANTOR shall at any time, by any means or ways, have, claim, or demand any right, title or interest in or to the aforesaid described premises or its appurtenances, or any rights thereof.

In WITNESS WHEREOF, the said _____ has hereunto set his _____ hand and affixed seal the day and year first above written.

Signed, sealed and delivered in presence of

(Amody)
Jerry Rager _____
Notary Public, Charlton County, Georgia
My Commission Expires Aug 17, 200_

R.L. Watts _____ (SEAL)
Ralph L. Watts _____ (SEAL)
_____ (SEAL)

Would you believe five (5) years later she told everyone she did not sign that deed.

We had to go down to Kingsland and get the lady to pull the record and verify her signature.

After they found out she lied; would you believe she told them I stole it. Isn't this Pitiful, huh?

For some reason she was always desperate for money. I mention to her often to have the children father take care of his children. As far as I know she went many years without child support for her children.

Why? Maybe love or fearful of what he might do. I believe she knew he was on dope and anything could happen.

I received an award for an accident. From this award for my aches and pains I gave her $3,158.38. Most of my award went into repairing my home.

Since this Rose received her profit sharing which was over $14,000. She didn't offer to pay the bank loan I borrowed for her auto accidents.

In January this year I promise to get this straighten out. I sent Rose Marie Harvey a letter on what we should do. She refused to answer.

One week later I sent her another letter; this one requesting her signature.

Some things were going wrong and I could not understand why.

Albertha Myers passed away October 26, 2000.

She had 0.37 acre of land

Albertha Newby (daughter) Executrix' Deed to herself March 21, 2001.

This deed is like the one Joe Jordan issued To Albirtha Turner October 10, 1951.

STATE OF GEORGIA
COUNTY OF CHARLTON

EXECUTRIX' DEED

THIS DEED, made this _21st_ day of March in the Year of Our Lord, Two Thousand One (2001), between ALBIRTHA F. NEWBY as Executrix of the last will and testament of ALBIRTHA J. MYERS (a/k/a ALBIRTHA JORDAN HARVEY and ALBIRTHA TURNER FARLOW HARVEY), late of the State of Georgia and County of Charlton, deceased, (the "Grantor") and ALBERTHA F. NEWBY (the "Grantee") of the State of Georgia and the County of Charlton; (Note that the terms: "Grantor" and "Grantee" include the respective heirs, successors and assigns where the context hereof requires or permits);

WITNESSETH THAT the Grantor (acting under and by virtue of the power and authority contained in the said will, the same having been duly probated and recorded in the Court of Probate of Charlton County, Georgia, for and in consideration of the sum of TEN dollars ($10.00 and other good and valuable consideration, in hand paid at and before the sealing and delivery of these presents, the receipt, adequacy and sufficiency of which being hereby acknowledged by the Grantor, has granted, bargained, sold and conveyed, and by these presents does hereby grant, bargain, sell and convey unto the Grantee, the following described real property:

All that tract or parcel of land lying and being in the 32nd. G. M. District of Charlton County, Georgia, more particularly described as follows: begin at the point which is the Southeast corner of the tract of land owned by Eliga Hannan, said corner being located along the Northern boundary of the right-of-way of the "Post Road" and from said point of beginning proceed in an Easterly direction along the said Northern boundary of the right-of-way of "Post Road" a distance of 130 feet to a point, then proceed in a Northerly direction a distance of 110 feet to a point, then proceed in a Westerly direction a distance of 130 feet to a point, then proceed in a Southerly direction along the property line of Eliga Hannan a distance of 110 feet back to the said point of beginning; said tract being bounded on the North by lands owned by Joe Jordan, on the East by lands owned by Willie V. Harvey, on the South by the Post Road, and on the West by lands owned by Eliga Hannan. References to private land ownership are as they presently exist or were formerly held.

TO HAVE AND TO HOLD the above-described tract or parcel of land, together with all and singular the rights, members and appurtenances thereof, to the same being, belonging, or in anywise appertaining to the only proper use, benefit, and behoof of the Grantee, forever, in FEE SIMPLE: in as full and ample a manner as the same was held, possessed, and enjoyed, or might have been held, possessed, and enjoyed, by the said deceased.

IN WITNESS WHEREOF, the Grantor has signed and sealed this Deed on the day and year first above written.

Signed, sealed and delivered in the presence of:

Albirtha Newby (SEAL)
ALBERTHA F. NEWBY, As Executrix
of the last Will and Testament
of ALBIRTHA J. MYERS (a/k/a ALBIRTHA JORDAN HARVEY
and ALBIRTHA TURNER FARLOW HARVEY)

_____
Unofficial Witness

_____
Notary Public
Notary Public Charlton County Georgia

This deed does not show the land Albirtha sold to Hanna.

49

The deed above is the original deed issued to Albirtha Farlow Myers as 110x130 which is 0.50 acre. Today it is not a 0.50 acre. She does not have a 110x130 acre. Albirtha Newby deed should reflex the 0.13 acre sold to Hanna.

I found out later that this deed should be 0.37 acres.

In the beginning it was a 0.50 acre but Albertha Myers sold 0.13 acre to the Hanna next door.

Charlton County Map #98A 11-28=95

,,,,,,,,,,,,,,

You can see plot #8 belongs to Albirtha Myers. It is 0.37 acre. Number 8 is using part of Elizabeth Jordan acre. This is where all the trouble begins.

I paid Robert Jordan $5,000.00 for Elizabeth Jordan acre and Albirtha Newby is using part of it.

Robert Jordan with his slick attorney issued me a deed for Lillie Mae Harvey land. This deed is phony and against the law to do such. I cannot have a phony deed recorded. It is against the law recording a phony deed. Knowing this deed is phony and having it recorded is against the law.

51

What has the law done about it? I told them I was issued a phony deed. Absolutely nothing; if I had given someone a phony deed; the police would come after me in the middle of the night.

The deed issued to Albirtha Newby is wrong. She does not have 110x130. She only have 0.37 acre. You have to wonder if people don't know any better or they do not have respect for the law. How do they expect to get away by doing this stuff?

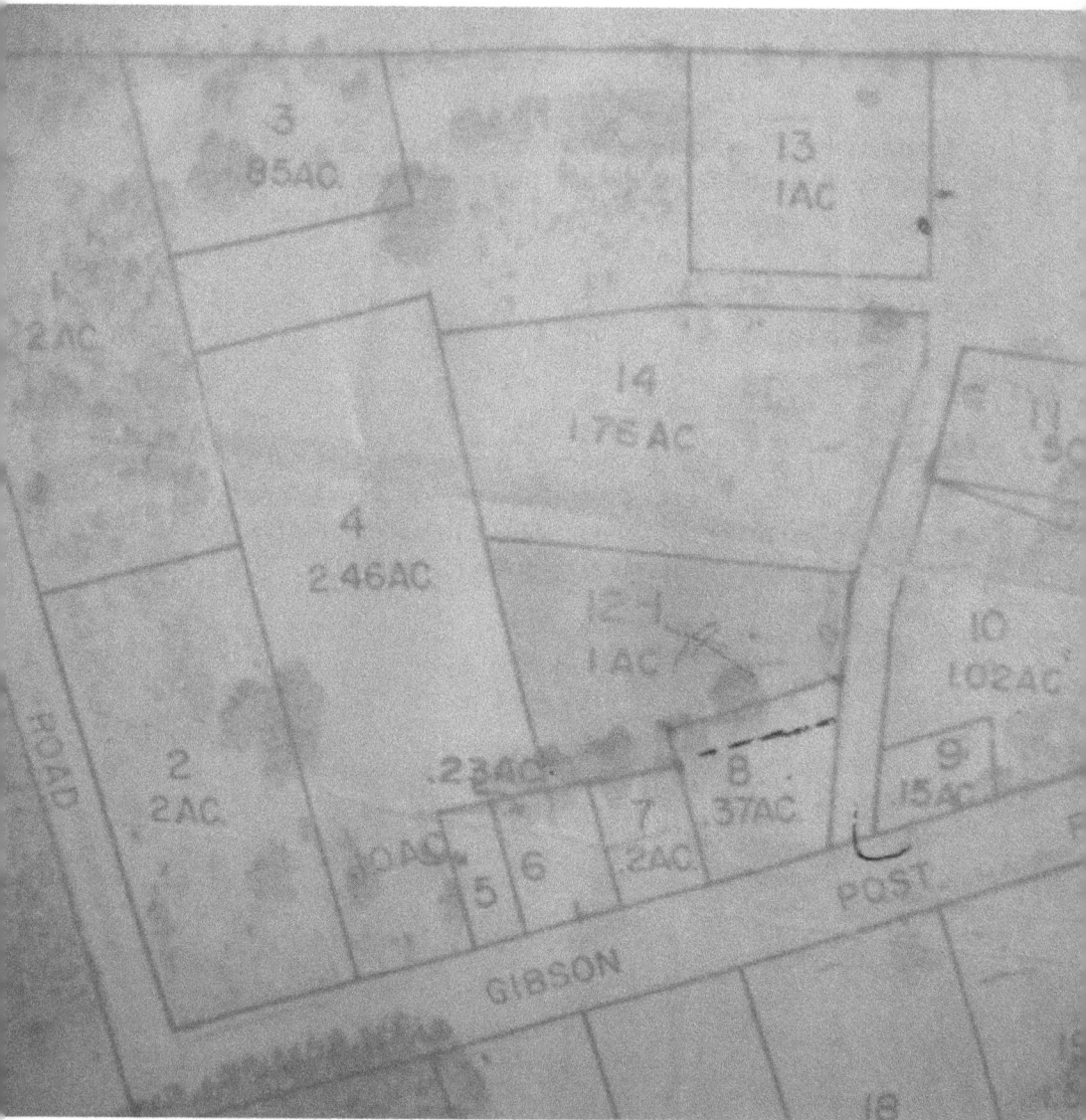

As you see the dotted line is part of my property. (Elizabeth Jordan)

53

I purchase Elizabeth Jordan acre and I cannot get the correct deed to this property. The acre is a 210x210 square. Myers now Newby claims that is her land. The Courts will not explain that she have less than an acre.

I went through Probate and paid $5,000.00 for Elizabeth Jordan acre.

Because the Newby's and Jordan's are friends they want to keep me from having what I paid for.

When I had my property surveyed they were all worried this would show up. Now, since I purchase Elizabeth Jordan acre from Robert Jordan the Administrator. They want me to forget about my deed to Elizabeth Jordan acre. Their plan was to scare me into signing this ugly document (phony deed) and pay them money.

This is so sad and sick. Why in the world people cannot be honest and live free of evil invocations? Refine and cultivate truths to make their lives fruitful. Initiate fruits to last for generations. Destroy Satan in your lives and gain a history of everlasting unforgettable fruits.

2000 was not a good year. Things began to happen and most are unbelievable. Hearing is great but when you see ugliness in an unpleasant manner is very distasteful.

I had this article printed in the Charlton County Herald for October 11, 2000. I had to because what I seen and heard am very awful and very, very ugly.

It is Vol. 104. No.4.Explanation will follow:

55

AS TIMES GOES BY....

By Ralph L. Watts

I named this *As times goes by* to speak of three difference times. Yesterday, today and tomorrow. Maybe not in that order.

Lets start with today. I moved here in the country approximately five years ago. Surrounded by religious families I argue this is the appropriate place for me. Pleased with the appearance of things I purchase an acre of land.

Months and months after the land purchase I could not get the information on where my land start or ends. Therefore I called a surveyor to find my property line. Here where the trouble begun. Some of the family came in a ficious manner objecting to the surveyor present. They also disputed the surveyor measurements. This was one of the most embarrassing moments in my life. The surveyor could not understand why they didn't want me to know where was my property line. This was the first.

The house across the street burns a lot of trash. Therefore there usually a fire burning trash everyday. This particular day I kept hearing small puppies cry. I didn't notice until I heard the lady next door yell "Take them puppies out that fire!" I ran to the front to notice one of the neighborhood boys running from the fire. One of the puppies died shortly; another died later. I asked some of my neighbors why not tell the parents? That was a no-no. They let me know immediately you don't tell that family anything about their kids. I were speechless. What type of kid would put a live animal in a fire? What type of parents would not accept information from other parents about their kids? Get the picture? Let's move on.

The second is about a dog. A man's best friend. Anywhere you go there are going to be problems. But when you have problems you sit down, discuss and debate various sides. You don't threaten or give expression of an intention to do harm to another. Okay let's get back to the dog.

One of the neighbors have a dog. A good looking dog to be exact. We also have children that must pass their house to get home. At first I thoughts the kids were exaggerating about being chase by this neighbor's dog. I watched to see for myself. The dog would growl and the kids would run with the dog in behind them. I went to the man of the house and explained what had happen. Surely the dog was tied for a day. A couple of days later their was another chase. This time one of the children fell in the bushes and her face received many scratches. Once again I went back to the neighbor's house. The man was not at home so I told his children to tell him to see me when he get home.

About an hour later I seen the neighbor coming down the road. I went to meet him so we could discuss what could be done about this situation. I could not believe what was happening. He came with a defiance attitude no one would believe. I could not discuss anything with him. I were force to call the authorities because I didn't want this to get out of hand.

I went back in my house and sat down. I had to think. As I sat there yesterday came before me. Most all my life I lived and worked around educators. I never had problems like this. Whenever a problem arose we were able to solve it. So I done some research around me. I found out why there are so many problems here.....

Let's go to tomorrow. Those who took the time to read this message; please if you have children keep them in school. Initiate in their minds the important of an education. Without it they will create unnecessary problems similar to mine. Let's recap on common sense. Everyone that owns property suppose to know where his property line. If you have a pet of any kind. That pet does not suppose to harm others. I have a fence. If I owned a dog behind my fence. If you come by and make an ugly face or yell at my dog and he come out and bite you. I am responsible for my animal. I must keep him contained. A person without an education might not know this. This is very difficult for some people.

I want to attach a piece of writing from a book I wrote around twenty years ago. The name of the book (now is being revised) The Futurity Race.

As Time Goes By

By Ralph L. Watts

I named this As times goes by to speak of three difference times. Yesterday, today and tomorrow; Maybe not in that order.

Lets start with today. I moved here in the country approximately five years ago. Surrounded by religious families I argue this is the appropriate place for me. Pleased with the appearance of things I purchase an acre of land.

Months and months after the land purchase I could not get the information on where my land start or ends. Therefore I called a surveyor to find my property line. Here is where the trouble begun. Some of the family came in a vicious manner objecting to the surveyor present. They also disputed the surveyor measurements. This was one of the most embarrassing moments in my life. The surveyor could not understand why they didn't want me to know where was my property line. This was the first.

The house across the street burns a lot of trash. Therefore there is usually a fire burning trash everyday. This particular day I kept hearing small puppies cry. I didn't notice until I heard the lady next door yell "Take them puppies out that fire!" I ran to the front to notice one of the neighborhood boys running from the fire.

One of the puppies died shortly; another died later. I asked some of my neighbors why not tell the parents? That was a no-no. They let me know immediately you don't tell that family anything about their kids. I was speechless. What type of kid would put a live animal in a fire? What type of parents would not accept information from other parents about their kids? Get the picture? Let's move on.

The second is about a dog. A man's best friend. Anywhere you go there are going to be problems. But when you have problems you sit down, discuss and debate various sides. You don't threaten or give expression of an intention to do harm to another. Okay let's get back to the dog.

One of the neighbors has a dog. A good looking dog to be exact. We also have children that must pass their house to get home. At first I thought the kids were exaggerating about being chase by this neighbor's dog. I watched to see for myself. The dog would growl and the kids would run with the dog in behind them. I went to the man of the house and explained what had happen. Surely the dog was tied for a day. A couple of days later their was another chase. This time one of the children fell in the bushes and her face received many

scratches. Once again I went back to the neighbor's house. The man was not at home so I told his children to tell him to see me when he get home.

About an hour later I seen the neighbor coming down the road. I went to meet him so we could discuss what could be done about this situation. I could not believe what was happening. He came with a defiance attitude no one would believe. I could not discuss anything with him. I was forced to call the authorities because I didn't want this to get out of hand.

I went back in my house and sat down. I had to think. As I sat there yesterday it came before me. Most all my life I lived and worked around educators. I never had problems like this. Whenever a problem arose we were able to solve it. So I done some research around me. I found out why there are so many problems here .

Let's go to tomorrow. Those who took the time to read this message; please if you have children keep them in school. Initiate in their minds the importance of an education. Without it they will create unnecessary problems similar to mine. Let's recap on common sense. Everyone that owns property suppose to know where his property line. If you have a pet of any kind. That pet is not suppose to harm others. I have a fence. If I owned a dog behind my fence. If you come by and make an ugly face or yell at my dog and he come out and bite you. I am responsible for my animal. I must keep him contained. A person without an education might not know this. This is very difficult for some people.

Letter to the Editor

Dear Editor,

I'd rather watch oatmeal bubble than endure another mind-numbing "me too" debate between Al Gore and George W. Bush. The major differences in them is the Democrat is for even larger government and abortion, while the Republican wants to maintain our already large government and is pro-life. So if these are the only candidates for President and you're not ...

included in the debates. If you don't have the time to write a letter then cut out this letter to the editor, sign your name to it and mail it to the above listed Commission.

E. Kevan Rowlee
P. O. Box 3031
Kingsland, GA 31548

That article was put in the paper because I wanted people to know something was going on.

Robert Jordan had two (2) young Boys living in his house. I was told they were his wife sister's children.

The lady that yelled "Take them dogs out the fire!" was Mrs. Buie who lived on the east side of Willie V and Lillie Mae Harvey. She could not stand to hear them puppies cry. When I heard it I could not believe it was happening.

Those kids put two puppies in the fire. Terrible isn't it; if you don't live here you would never know things could be so wrong. How in the world can anyone; child or adult throw a small puppy in a fire? One died then and the other died later. I am convinced there are serious problems here.

Everyone was afraid to go and tell Robert about these two boys. I guess they thought and he wanted them to think he was monstrous.

Lillie Mae Harvey usually burn trash everyday.

Robert Jordan later got a beautiful black dog with a very pretty coat. This is the dog that chased the children.

I tried to speak with him about the dog. He came down the road cursing, etc.

I told him I do not wish to speak with him anymore. I had to call the police to calm him down.

Now I knew there were many serious problems out here on Bear Mountain. Maybe I was trying to ignore them because I lived out there.

One day at Southeastern Bank a bank officer approached me.

She asked me where I live and did I print this article? (As Times Goes By.) I told her where I live and yes I printed the article.

She paused and looked at me in a serious way and said "You be careful out there!" Now I do think and believe there are serious problems.

February 9, 2000 I made an agreement to loan Mr. Harvey
$400.00

I often had to help Willie V. Harvey pay the taxes on his land. No
other family member would help.

At one time Mr. Harvey had to pay taxes on three (3) parcels.
This time I paid the tax on one of the parcels for him and loan
him $400.00 to pay on the other two.

AGREEMENT

Tuesday, February 29, 2000

THIS IS AN AGREEMENT BETWEEN RALPH L. WATTS AND
WILLIE V. HARVEY.
RALPH L. WATTS AGREE TO LOAN WILLIE V. HARVEY
$400.00. THIS MONEY IS
TO BE PAID BACK AT $100.00 PER MONTH THE FIRST
PAYMENT IS DUE ON THE
FIRST OF APRIL. (April 01, 2000) THE LAST PAYMENT IS DUE
THE FIRST OF JULY.
(July 01, 2000) THIS MONEY WAS ISSUED ON CHECK #0452
SOUTHEASTERN BANK.

THIS AGREEMENT MUST BE SIGNED BY BOTH PARTIES.

_____

RALPH L. WATTS

_____

WILLIE V. HARVEY

_____

61

Rose wanted me to pay this bill for her. I never did understand
where these folks did with their money. I do understand Mr.
Harvey and wife did not have much money coming in so I tried to
help them.

I refused to pay because this was not working or helping.

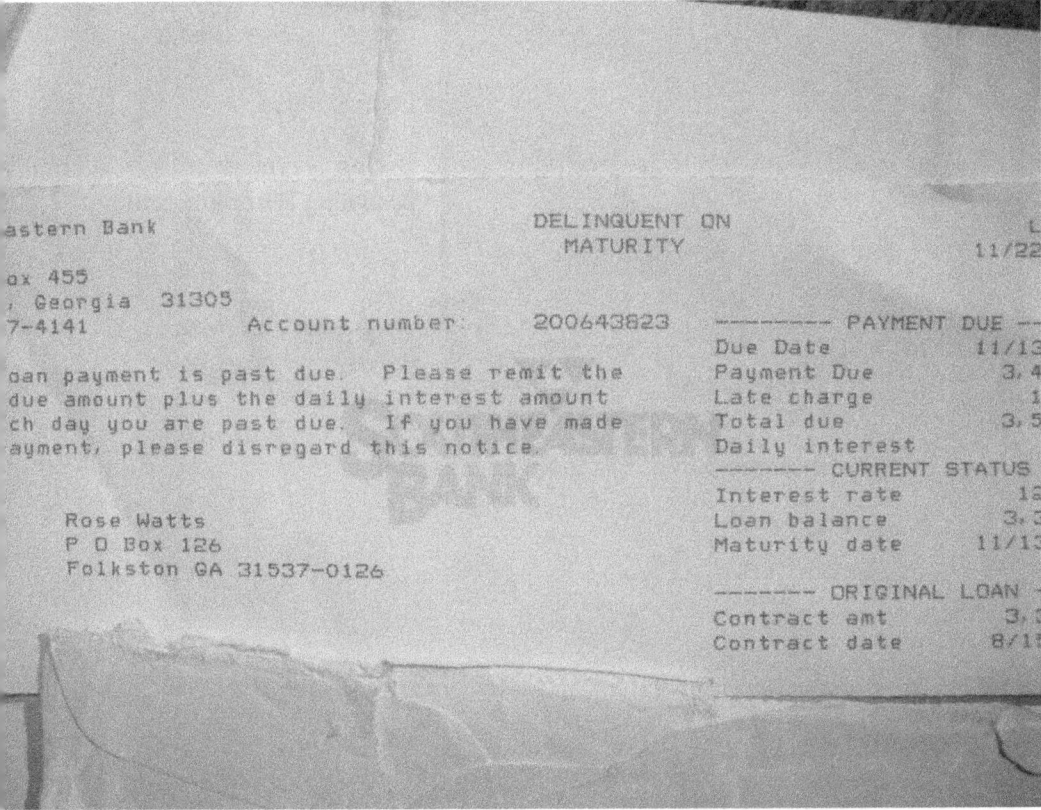

```
astern Bank                        DELINQUENT ON              L
                                   MATURITY                   11/22

ox 455
; Georgia  31305
7-4141            Account number:   200643823    ------- PAYMENT DUE --
                                                 Due Date        11/13
oan payment is past due.  Please remit the       Payment Due      3.4
due amount plus the daily interest amount        Late charge       1
ch day you are past due.  If you have made       Total due        3.5
ayment, please disregard this notice.            Daily interest
                                                 ------- CURRENT STATUS
                                                 Interest rate       12
     Rose Watts                                  Loan balance       3.3
     P O Box 126                                 Maturity date   11/13
     Folkston GA 31537-0126
                                                 ------- ORIGINAL LOAN -
                                                 Contract amt       3.3
                                                 Contract date     8/1
```

December 27, 2000 Lillie Mae executed Security Deed to Fremont Investment and Loan

when this loan was executed.

April 19, 2001 Lillie Mae and Willie Executed a Secure deed to S & S Loan Service.

Still no one mention probating Elizabeth acre.

Whenever Lillie Mae Harvey would get a Secured Deed it was mostly for 12.52 acres. That includes part of Elizabeth Jordan acre.

63

ROSE M. HARVEY WATTS

    Plaintiff

    vs.

RALPH LEON WATTS

    Defendant

{   CIVIL ACTION NO. 03V-9(
{
{
{
{
{
{
{

ANSWER AND COUNTERCLAIM

COMES NOW, RALPH LEON WATTS, the Defendant in the above-
action and files this his Answer and Counterclaim to Plaintif
Complaint For Divorce and shows the Court the following, to-w

1.

The Defendant admits the allegations contained in Paragr
and 2 of Plaintiff's Complaint.

2.

The Defendant denies the allegations contained in Parag:
of Plaintiff's Complaint and further shows that upon informa'
that he has received Defendant believes that the Plaintiff w
married to Kenneth Reed and that she and Mr. Reed never divo:

3.

Responding to Paragraphs 4, 5, 6, and 7 of Plaintiff's
Complaint Defendant shows that as the parties were not and a:
married as set forth herein; the said paragraphs require no

On April 2003 I received a Divorce Summons.

64

A complaint for divorce stating we separated the 20th of December, 2002. We separated before I moved out her house. The latter part of 1995 and first of 1996 while staying in her house we were not speaking. The only time she would speak is when she wants to borrow money.

This lady hasn't spoken to me but once since 12/31/01. That was the day I learned she was using the children's daddy last name. She asked me to pay $62.00 on her Sears account. The name on the account is Mrs. Rose H. Reed. The next time she sent me a note by one of her children to loan her $40.00.

The Summon states the plaintiff wants to be granted the marital home. What marital home? She still lives in her house. We never had a home together. Does she mean the house she signed over to me?

Rose forgot she had sold and deeded me her part of the acre.

This house began to look good and she wants to be a gold digger. If she wants a new home she should ask her children's father (Her legal husband) to provide a home for them. That's what I done for my children. I am restoring this raggedy house with my award money and she is not entitled to one cent.

65

Anybody with any common sense can see what is going on. I really hate for someone to know Rose was this dirty. I think she is being coach by someone who doesn't know Rose have signed this house to me in 1999. Nor do they know about common-law marriages.

I tried years ago to get Rose to set these names straight. Now she waits until I fix this old house (house she signed over to me) and wants to jump back in the picture.

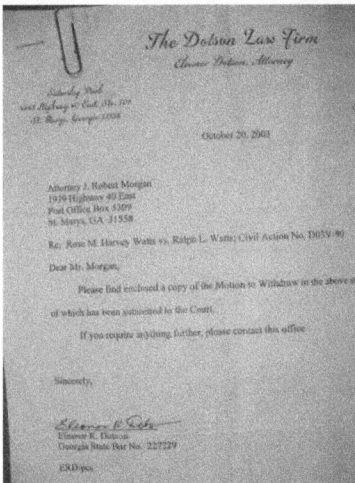

I should not have to ask for the house I live in and restoring. It is already mind because she signed it to me. What I do ask that this marriage be null and void. I have proven she was using her children father's name. (Legally married)

I ask the Court for Rose to pay me 6,158.38. $3,000.00 is ½ of the bank loan she agreed to pay. $3,158.38 is the money she got from me when I received my award. (She received $14,000 profit sharing after my award)

THE SUPERIOR CORUT FOR THE COUNTY
OF CHARLTON, STATE OF GEORGIA

ROSE M. HARVEY WATTS   [CIVIL ACTION NO. 2003-SU-CV-90
                                 [
    PLAINTIFF   [
                                 [
        VS   [
                                 [
RALPH LEON WATTS   [
                                 [
    DEFENDANT   [

FINAL JUDGMENT AND DECREE

With this case having come before the Court on the 1st day of February, 200⁵

at Calendar Call and there being no appearance by the Plaintiff and upon the Motion

of Defendant; IT IS ORDERED that the Plaintiff's Complaint for Divorce is hereby

dismissed.

IT IS FURTHER ORDERED that Defendant's Counterclaim for Annulment is

granted and it is hereby ordered that the marriage between the parties is hereby

annulled and declared to be void and of no effect. The status of the parties is deemed

to be as if the purported marriage had never been contracted or attempted.

And it is considered, ordered and decreed by the Court that the marriage

contract heretofore entered into between the parties to this case, from and after this

67

date, be and is set aside and dissolved as fully and effectually as if no such contract

had ever been made or entered into, and Plaintiff and Defendant, in the future shall

be held and considered as separate and distinct persons altogether unconnected by

any nuptial union or civil contract whatsoever, and both shall have the right to

remarry.

SO ORDERED, ADJUDGED AND DECREED this the ___1___ day of

_____, 2005, nunc pro tunc the ___ ay of February, 2005.

_____
STEPHEN L. JACKSON
CHIEF JUDGE
SUPERIOR COURT
CHARLTON COUNTY, GEORGIA
WAYCROSS JUDICIAL CIRCUIT

Order prepared by:

_____
J. Robert Morgan
Attorney for Defendant
State Bar No. 0522650
P. O. Box 5309
St. Marys, GA 31558
(912) 576-5615 – Phone
(912) 576-5617 – Facsimile

68

I also ask the Court to instruct Rose, her children, family and friends not to be offensive to me or my property.

When this is done we can live happy forever.

Rose back out and refused everything. If she could not get any money she didn't do anything.

I went to The Dotson Law Firm and explained our marriage and what Rose was trying to do. Rose just lied about everything and make those lies sound convincing. Boy! She was good at it; you just cannot pick that up everyday.

When they learned what was going on and the lies Rose told they dropped the case. They withdrew because it was an embarrassing to try and defend a lie.

Back at the house I continue fixing and replacing.

I had to replace all the windows and doors. I replace the roof and had the wiring redone. I replace fixtures and half fix the bathroom. Within four years this old house began to take shape. The neighbors began to watch.

One day I came home and I had no water. I went outside and check the pipe that led water to the house. I saw where someone had broken the pipe. A neighbor across the street told me the lady next door stomped the pipe and broke it. I knew she was mean and ugly but this is extreme and I did not think no one would go this far.

I called a mechanic and had the well fixed. When the well was being repaired; this neighbor and Robert Jordan wife would sit and watch. The impressions they gave were I was not suppose to be able to fix this.

I also had the surveyors to survey my land. While during their job some neighbors would talk loud to let them know their surveying was wrong.

I ask the Surveyors not to pay them any attention.

July 16, 2003 I had to file a civil complaint against Robert Jordan and Dan Newby. They had got to the point where I could not come out my door without some ugly things going on. (Copy enclosed) I just wanted to be left along; why wouldn't they leave me along?

They were annoying, aggravating and just plain disgraceful. I was really tired of them. Like they had nothing to do but watch me.

71

IN THE MAGISTRATE COURT OF CHARLTON COUNTY
STATE OF GEORGIA   Court telephone: 912-496-2617

NOTICE OF TRIAL

Case no: **Civil Complaint**

PLAINTIFF: **Ralph L Watts**

ATTORNEY: NONE ON RECORD

PO Box 36
Folkston, GA 31537

ATTORNEY: NONE ON RECORD

-vs-

DEFENDANT: Robert James Jordon

Rt 2 Box 4098
Folkston, GA 31537

An answer having been filed by the Defendant, your case has been scheduled for trial on
  July 23 2003   at   10:00 AM   , to be held at the Magistrate Court Building located at 100B
County Street, Folkston, Georgia.

You will receive NO further notice. If your case is settled before trial, you will NEED to dismiss this
case in writing.

CERTIFICATE OF SERVICE

Both parties (and attorney's of record, if any) have been notified of court date, time and location
by the United States Mail, with adequate postage affixed.

July 16 2003

APPROPRIATE DRESS REQUIRED
NO SHORTS! NO HATS!
NO SUNGLASSES!

CLERK / DEPUTY CLERK

72

IN THE MAGISTRATE COURT OF CHARLTON COUNTY
STATE OF GEORGIA

NOTICE OF TRIAL

Re: Civil Complaint

PLAINTIFF Ralph L Watts

ATTORNEY   NONE ON RECORD

PO Box 36
Folkston, GA 31537

ATTORNEY   NONE ON RECORD

vs

DEFENDANT Danny Newby and
Alberta Newby

Rt 2 Box 6090
Folkston, GA 31537

As answer has been filed by the Defendant, your case has been scheduled for trial on ___ July 23 2003 ___ at ___ 10:00 AM ___ to be held at the Magistrate Court Building located at 1005 County Street, Folkston, Georgia.

You will receive NO further notice. If your case is settled before trial, you will NEED to dismiss this case in writing.

CERTIFICATE OF SERVICE

Both parties (and attorneys of record, if any) have been notified of court date, time and location by the United States Mail with adequate postage affixed.

July 16 2003

APPROPRIATE DRESS REQUIRED
NO SHORTS; NO HATS;
NO SUNGLASSES

CLERK / DEPUTY CLERK

73

I received another message from Rose for a loan. I believe this woman just burns money. After all I have gone through with her it would seem like she would be ashamed. No not Rose she was not ashamed of anything.

Below is the letter to her:

Monday, November 24, 2003

Hello Rose,

I see you still use the word "loan". The word loan means to pay back. I'm still paying on your loan from Southeastern Bank. Remember the car accident. Yes, I'm still paying on that bill. I rather hear the word give than loan.

When you speak of your granddaddy's house, this was not a house when I moved here. It was something I would not keep my dog in. My money into this shack made it look better now and everyone wants to say my daddy or granddaddy's house.

I have checks where I paid your daddy for this property. He also knew when the last payment was made. It is not my responsibility to make sure he shares this information with his wife. (This I found out in later years, information was not shared).

What I want from you is the truth. Tell people the truth or tell them to butt out. People come to me about the printing in the newspaper. If you read it, you should know I didn't say anything about you. A few guys that really don't know me always tell me my wife is going with some guy. The letter was to them. "If that's what happening you take her home". The letter didn't say anything about Rose Harvey or Rose Watts. I'm telling these guys if this woman is running with all these men, they should take her home. I didn't expect some to understand but you I did. You fell right in their trap. They needed someone to help them exercise their ugliness.

What happens to us is our business. You know how you feel about me. I know how I feel about you. Even though it hurts so badly I have to say I'll always love you. I love clean living and know what it takes to get around Satan. A person has to carry himself/herself in a way to keep respect and not allow Satan to come into their lives.

Many of your friends were afraid we might make things great in our lives. They were right if you would have listened to me. Not someone telling you I am trying to <u>control</u> you. Thank about it- How can I control you when I'm trying to make life better for you and your family.

I'm still shocked you didn't know better. Maybe the one told you this you loved them better. If controlling me will make my life better!! You better believe I want to be controlled.

About the money there have to be some discussions. Maybe one day when you find time you'll call or meet me to discuss this matter.

I enclosed a letter which I hope to release soon. You can be the first to read it. By this letter you can see there is love for everybody.

The last thing I want to tell you is about your son Kenneth Junior (June). A few days ago he left riding with Jarvis.

When they passed my house I looked up. When I looked at the car passing June hollowed out at me in an ugly way. Now I don't know what's going on in your daddy's house. But I will not tolerate or endure foolishness from children. June might treat them anyway does not give him the right to harass me over here.

I remember some time ago I went over to your dad's house. June was on the couch. I spoke to June and he didn't say anything. Your daddy tried to tell him that wasn't nice. I told your Father to not try to make him speak to me-everything is ok.

I don't ever intend to interfere with his thoughts. If he is that angry-he is going to be angry by himself. But there is a law against harassment. Please let him know I am not like his granddad. I love him but harassments are out.

Understanding,

Ralph L. Watts

Sunday, March 04, 2004

To WHOM THIS MAY CONCERN

This open letter is to a few people who took upon themselves to exercise ugliness and offensive to me and my property.

It really sad some people grow old without learning the value of life. A behavior problem of jealousy exists and the only way you know to fight back is with hate and greed. You possess this element of inferior quality which creates a heavy burden. A heavy burden makes one <u>undesirable</u>, <u>repulsive</u> and <u>untrustworthy</u>. Then he becomes confined in a state of <u>hate</u>, <u>greed</u> and <u>animosity.</u>

I find reasons for some of the jealousy behavior. It so many that perceives education is not a factor in their lives. An education <u>disciplines</u>, <u>cultivates</u> and <u>train</u> your mind. One man was at my house and expressed his feelings about education. "Education don't hold value in a person's life" When I heard this I realize I was with the wrong person. I gradually moved from his company.

Another person took up the banner describing I had a desire to date her. What an erroneous idea!!! I educated (degreed) all my children and their mother. What in the world would I do with an uneducated woman? I said something nice because I thought you was going into business. I love to see women in the business field. Education is what I preach. No dear, just because I try to be polite and courteous doesn't constitute request for a date.

I tell all people I love them. I love the lady that stomped and broke my water pipe. I love the lady that pulled up my surveyor's stake. All the lies that were told on me, I love the teller. God said <u>vengeance</u> is mine. All that was done I do not wish to retaliate. Never-the-less I have to say I still love you.

Naturally I have a repugnance attitude for this type of behavior and care not to ever congregate.

Ralph L. Watts

PS. Don't just sit around and talk about people. Find a girl friend or boy friend. Choose a hobby! Go fishing! Do something constructive!!!!!
March 2004 I had this article printed in the local paper

In September of 2004 I happen to look at the ads in the local newspaper.

Here where I read that Robert Jordan is claiming and trying to be the Administrator of Elizabeth Jordan acre. I had no notice that his Attorney was or anything from the Courts. I had until September 9th to answer.

These people will not quit. They continue to hound me every day. I

guess because they need money and trying to get it anyway they can.

79

GARY A. BACON

Attorney and Counselor at Law
100 Mariners Drive, Suite C
Kingsland, Georgia 31548

Telephone 912 882-7322   Email: gbacon@usa.com
Facsimile   912 882-8017   Website: baconlawfirm.com

November 23, 2004

Honorable Robert F. Phillips
Judge of the Probate Court
Charlton County Courthouse
100 South 3rd Street
Folkston, Georgia 31537

Dear Judge Phillips:

Re: Legal Representation of Robert Jordan, Petitioner and the Elizabeth Jordan Estate

Please be advised that I represent Mr. Robert Jordan in his legal matter before the
Charlton County Probate Court.

Sincerely,

Gary A. Bacon

Later that month on the 23rd I receive this notice from Gary Bacon that
he was Robert Jordan's Attorney.

81

I thought that would help but things got worst. He got the idea that my land was his mother's and he wanted to be the Administrator of his mother's estate. His mother had no estate. There was only an acre of land.

October 15 2004 I hired Henry & Associates of Kingsland, GA to survey my Property again. Someone had moved the surveyor's to where they wanted them. I cannot believe people would do this, well; again I was warned at the grocery store about my neighbors.

82

HENRY & ASSOCIATES
Reg. Land Surveyors
P.O. Box 1236

(912)
729-5540

97 S. Clarks Bluff Rd.
Kingslands, GA 31548

Fax Number
729-2436

TO NAMS, RALPH C.

PARTIAL PAYMT.

1 AC @ BEAR MOUNT. FOLKST.

$ 250⁰⁰

STATEMENT   TERMS   DATE 10-15-04

DATE	DESCRIPTION	AMOUNT
	PREVIOUS BALANCE	
10-15-04	PARTIAL PAYMT. 1 AC. BOUNDARY SURVEY @ BEAM MOUNTAIN RD FOLKSTON GA.	$250⁰⁰
10-15-04	PAID PARTIAL PAYMT.	

PREVIOUS BAL	CHARGES		PAYMENTS	NEW BALANCE
DUE	P/AL. WHEN DWG DONE			$150⁰⁰

HENRY & ASSOCIATES

The day they surveyed some family members booed and made statements like the Surveyors did not know what they were doing.

I ask the Surveys to please continue and not pay any attention to them.

Do you see? Here are grown-ups acting like kids in a crazy mode. Get the picture?

When we all went before Judge Philips and I explain to all. The property that Elizabeth Jordan owned was non-existed at this time. I even drew an outline of my property and also Elizabeth Jordan property. Judge Phillips knew there was a problem because we were discussing two different parcels.

I also explain the clerks at the Court House searched the court records and did not find a house or aerial shot of the acre that Elizabeth Jordan owned.

After all this and the evidence presented Judge Phillips assign Robert Jordan Administrator without any questions. This was the beginning of my fate.

Elizabeth Jordan acre is a 210 ft square. The property I owned is not a 210 ft square. If Lillie Mae Harvey was not allowed to redraw lines it should have not been accepted by her family or the companies she mortgage the land with.

No one had any problems until Robert Jordan jealously got an attorney to persuade Judge Phillips to place me in this ridiculous position

Now some twenty or thirty years later they want me to pay for land the Mortgage companies owned. I really cannot believe attorneys would stoop so low. Everyone should know this isn't right.

The attorneys pulled this trick hoping by me being an old man they can get by. I will continue to pursue this and ask my children to do the same. I want the world to know what happen here. I want the world to know how an ugly decision took all my retirement savings. How an ugly decision cause me to get in a state of depression.

Everything Lillie Mae Harvey done was accepted by her family and the courthouse officials.

Robert's attorney argues that he is entitling to his mother's estate. Robert probably told his attorney all those repairs and additions I done are his mother's estate.

There was no estate. There was only an acre of land. How can you make someone Administrator of an acre of land which cost about $2,000.00 at that time?

I took this case to three Law firms and they said it was ashamed the Probate Judge didn't stop this. After some thirty years passed; the parcels mortgage and re-mortgage and the old house was no good. The only thing left was an acre of land. To call this an estate is against all the laws of any Court.

I had to tell them the Probate Judge didn't know I rebuild the property and made it live-able. My attorney (which did nothing) supposes to introduce this at the trial. (Which never happen?)

I do not know if Robert's Attorney knew the truth. All Robert's attorney seen was my finish work. Robert probably told him he built his mother's house and he kept the property up. His mother did this work. He already told the Court many lies.

I think about all these brilliant minds and hands these papers went through.

No one caught anything but Honorable Judge Jackson. I believe he looks at the presentation and it didn't look good.

86

Therefore he refused to rule and told those attorneys to go to trial. It didn't look good to them either; that is the reason I am writing this book. They coerce me into signing a document that wasn't Court presentable. (This should not be aloud).

I recognized some trouble in the beginning. There was this Court Reporter at the meeting. I did not know anything about her present until I arrive. After the meeting Ann Rewis (Court Reporter) asked me to pay half of her fee. I asked how much was her fee? She told me $90.00 which mean I had to pay $45.00.

Ann Rewis sent me a bill for $90.00. Why would she send me a bill for the total amount? That meant that Robert's attorney did not have to pay his part.

On February 25, 2005 I sent the payment under protest. ((letter enclosed) I said if she made a mistake I would receive my half back.

I did not hear from her or receive a copy of the proceedings. I suppose they got together and laugh at the deal they had pulled on me.

An online attorney said I should have gotten a copy of that meeting. I ask myself why people do these things. They are Professionals and their jobs tell people who they are.

She owes me $45.00 plus 8% from February 2005 and a copy of the proceedings.

I had so I wrote Robert Jordan attorney.

Tuesday, December 16, 2008

Gary A. Bacon, Atty.

Post Office Box 5880

St. Marys, Georgia 31558

I have a right by law to get what I pay for.

Friday, February 25, 2005

To: Ann Rewis   RE: Petition of Robert Jordan
    P. O. Box 20601   Charlton Probate Court
    Saint Simons Island, Georgia

Ms. Rewis,

requested to participate in this hearing by Judge Phillip.

did not request or knew a Court Reporter was necessary. If I had know
eporter was necessary
 would have contacted my attorney and an agreement would take place
Never-the-less I was told by you at the hearing the cost would be fifty
($50.00) dollars. Now I received a bill for ninety $90.00) dollars which se
 am paying the whole bill.

A check is sent to you for that amount under protest. There is no known
eason why I should pay this amount.

Under Protest,

Ralph L. Watts

When Judge Philips made Robert Jordan Administrator of Elizabeth Jordan acre of land everything made a 180 degree turn. Robert Jordan process the weapon he wanted to get money from me.

One attorney told me this whole thing should have been investigated before making such a serious decision. Making someone Administrator is an awful weapon especially if the person is not a responsible person. Robert Jordan is not a responsible person. Remember I just took him to Civil Court for harassments. This is really awful.

If there would have been an investigation; the investigators would learned that Robert Jordan was trouble before then. I had filed a Civil Suite about his activities in July 2003.

I needed some answers right away: I placed this ad in a paper hoping to get some information.

Searching for answers

Searching for answers: I live in Georgia: The Story: Long ago a man purchase sixteen (16) acres of land. He deeded an (one) acre (210 sq ft) to his wife.

Later his wife dies. Later he got sick himself and only one of his children (out of approx.7 children) would help him. He then deeds all the sixteen acres plus one acre (17) seventeen acres to the child that took care of him.

Lillie Mae Harvey cared for all the lands, paying taxes, etc, for twenty years. In this twenty years process difference family members purchase or took up resident on this land. The one acre deed to her mother from her father (210 sq ft) wasn't there anymore. The lands had been rearranged to forfeit the 210 sq acres without a deed to substantiate the changed.

I purchase an acre about nine years ago. The acre is near the one acre that was deeded to her mother. My acre description is totally different. The other family waits until I build this property up and they are saying this acre belongs to the children of their mother. (210 sq ft acre)

My acre has only 85 ft on one side; totally different from the 210 sq ft acre. If some have any ideas of cases like this in any court or what would they do in a case like this;

PLEASE!! PLEASE!! Help ASAP. I really appreciate your help or answers.

Thanks again,

ralphwatts@comcast.net

I knew I had to do something. I was very depressed; I would catch myself going to sleep with a terrible headache. I knew my blood pressure was rocketing. I had to go home and rest for a day.

The next day I went looking for an attorney. I knew attorneys here in Folkston knew the Harvey and Jordan families. Therefore I went to Waycross to look for an Attorney.

I didn't know much about Waycross but I knew where the Courthouse was located. Down from the Court House was this good looking building with an Attorney name on it.

McGee and McGee Law Firm

I went in an asked the clerk for an Attorney. She first said no one is in then she pause and said "Attorney McGee is in the back" She made a call to the back and I was told to come on back.

I walked and seen this elderly man sitting behind his desk. The first thing came to my mind is this man is too old or he is a great attorney.

We introduce ourselves and I explain my problems. He seem like he knew and would do a lots for me. This made me feel better because I knew a little explanation in a Court of Law I would prevail. I accepted him for my attorney.

Civil Action # 05V-0228

I want to add a few items in the Plaintiff portion of the pretrial order draft:

The following is the Plaintiff's Brief and Succinct outline of the case and contentions:

Elizabeth Jordan has a single family home which was built by the administrator of the estate who is her son.

The above statement is a lie. That is the reason why I ask my attorney to interview Willie V. Harvey. Willie V. stated to me Robert Jordan was a DRUNK. Joe Jordan had her built by Jim Walter Corp; office in Tampa, FL

He also stated the current occupant; Ralph L. Watts is stubbornly litigious and acting in bad faith and without substantial justification in opposing efforts to obtain the property.

Why did I have to have a Civil Complaint against him and Dan Newby?

Do you see how easy for him to lie! He is the one with all this ugliness.

I never did anything to anyone since I met Rose and came there in 1994. He is just a jealous and a hunger something.

He stated also due to threats made by Mr. Watts and subsequently a threatened loss of rents, Mr. Watts should be accompanied by a law enforcement official when on the premises.

When I read this I said I know Robert don't know any better but his attorney should have more respect for himself than to print something like this.

This case was full of lies. It is against the law for anyone to file a notarized copy in courts of law that are lies.

Robert told the Court I knew his mother in 1977. I didn't meet Rose until 1994. That is seventeen years later when I first came to Folkston, GA. The guy is way off; he cannot tell a lie that is close.

I did not know anyone who lives in Folkston. He lied about he built his mother's house. He lied about his mother's estate. The house I rebuilt and additions to the property he claims it was his mother's estate.

During the time Joe Jordan built Elizabeth Jordan house Robert was a regular drunk.

Everyone I meet that knew Robert back in the day say he was just out there.

His attorney or Judge Philips probably did not know. These lies should not be allowed in any Court of Law.

What happen now? If the Courts believe there were fraud in Filed notarized court documents; they would order the plaintiff to prove before the court that these arguments are false.

The trouble makers out on Bear Mountain are the Newby's and Robert Jordan. All my troubles came with these two in the middle.

His sister was down sick and he does not visit but he runs to his mother-in-law. Get the picture!!!!!.

He was told by one of his nieces when they mother die do not come around.

This happen a few months ago in 2012)

I want you to read part of the Court documents that was presented:

WHEREFORE, Plaintiff prays for:

1) Immediate possession of the property;

2) That the Defendant be restrained from coming on the property without supervision of law enforcement officials;

3) That a judgment be entered awarding Plaintiff rent in the amount of $10,800.00

4) That a judgment be entered striking the illegal deeds which have be filed;

5) That a judgment be entered which finds that fee simple legal title is in the title Elizabeth Jordan, intestate;

6) That reasonable attorney fees and the costs of this action be awarded against Defendant; and

7) That the Court grant such other relief as it deems necessary.

This _15th_ day of August, 2005.

Respectfully submitted,

Gary A. Bacon
Attorney for Plaintiff
Georgia State Bar No. 030713

This document says the deed Lillie Mae Harvey issued me is illegal.

Therefore if her deed is illegal then you must go back to the original deed.

The original deed is 210x210 sq. Come on please do not play dumb.

August 26, 2005 I received notice of a non-jury trial date set for September 6, 2005 at 10.00 o'clock am. This is before Honorable Judge Stephen L. Jackson.

On September 6, 2005 my attorney was a little late but got there time enough to speak in my defense.

I could not hear what they said but Honorable Stephen L. Jackson sent this case to Jury trial. I always wanted to personal thank him for that. He seems like a very honorable man.

Now I was satisfied with the way this case is going; to trial I might add.

This is the best feeling I had since this case started; I just knew we could win because the presentation was inadequate.

On September 9, 2005 I sent my attorney this letter to my attorney.

Dear Mr. McGee,

Once again I want to say thanks for accepting me as one of your clients.

Every now and then I might hear something I think would be valuable to our case. I would like permission to send this information or drop papers off at your office.

Meanwhile at the Post Office yesterday one of his (Robert Jordan) not-so-close- friends approached me. Around town Robert is bragging if he goes to court he is sure to win. He is a life long resident of Folkston and I'm not.

I know you understand what he can or cannot do. Still this is scary for me. I'm not sure if we can have the case moved to Ware County. I do trust and believe you will make the right decision.

Once again I do thank you for your help in this urgent matter.

Sincerely,

Ralph L. Watts

J. BAKER McGEE, JR.
JAMES BAKER McGEE, III

February 7, 2006

Mr. Ralph Watts
P.O. Box 36
Folkston GA 31537

Dear Mr. Watts,

Enclosed is a copy of a letter I received today from Gary Bacon. If y
a price you may. If you do not, please call for an appointment and lets g
ready for trial.

Sincerely yours,

McGee and McGee, P.C.

J. Baker McGee, Jr.

JBM/las

Enclosure (s)

I got a message that they wanted to buy my property

Below is the letter I sent to him.

February 12, 2006

Dear Mr. Baker;

I received your letter and the copy from Mr. Bacon. I really think Robert Jordan is giving his attorney the wrong information.

They approached me about selling my property. He asked me twice and his sister in Miami, FL left her number on my answering service to call her. She is the one told me Robert was not going to continue because of money shortage. **NO I DO NOT WANT TO SELL MY PROPERTY**.

I want to continue to litigate this matter. All his lies will come out in a court of law.

I will call Monday maybe we can set some dates to meet for this trail.

Thank you,

Ralph L. Watts

My children said I should get another attorney because this one is speaking about you loosing everything. They said either he does not know what to do or he is going to sell you out.

On March 4, 2006 I sent my attorney this letter:

I wanted to make sure at this trial everything went OK

Saturday, March 04, 2006

J. Baker McGee, Jr.
313 Albany Avenue
P.O. Drawer 679
Waycross, GA 31502-0679

Dear Mr. Baker,

RE: Robert J. Jordan vs. Ralph L. Watts

I am still collecting information on the money I spent for this property.

I found out I am losing because all the labor put into this place. I look for another place to live; unfortunately, I cannot afford another house. Things are just too high for the money I am receiving.

101

I spoke with my children and they gave me an idea. They are willing to pay for another Attorney because their idea is two heads are better than one. They are willing to pay your son if the both of you can save my property. Therefore, I am begging you to help me. Let me know if this is a good idea to enlist your son in this case.

In purchasing this property I thought I done things right. In 1995, I spent a long time in the tax office checking this property. The clerks hope me and we came up with the same information. The deed from Joe Jordan to his wife does not exist. The description on Joe Jordan deed and my property does not match. We could not find the description of Joe Jordan deed anywhere on the property map. This alone told me it ok to purchase this property.

Never the less when Rose (granddaughter) and I purchase this property it was ok. When they found out Rose had sold me her interest; they wanted it back. There is something wrong with this picture.

I do appreciate if you can help me in this urgent matter.

Sincerely yours,

Ralph L. Watts

I did not get an answer from him. That was frightening; my children beg me to get another attorney. This one is not going to help me. I had a feeling my children are right. "Daddy this attorney is not going to help you, please get another attorney".

They were very serious.

I place an ad hoping I can get another attorney:

This letter below was placed March 19, 2006 among groups of attorneys

Sunday, March 19, 2006

Dear Sir or Madam:

I want to apologize for this message but please help me with answers if you can.

Let start from the beginning: Joe Jordan purchase seventeen (16) acres from let say Bill some Seventy years ago. He divorced his wife shortly afterward. He gave her a deed for one acre of land from the sixteen. He builds a house on this one acre. Later she passed and Joe Jordan continues to live well.

Later Joe Jordan got sick. He had about four or five children. Only one of his children came to take care of him. Let us say her name is Lillie Mae. Lillie Mae took care of her father for many years until he died. Before he died, he made a deed for seventeen acres to Lillie Mae.

Lillie Mae did not have any money. Therefore, she asked her sisters and brothers if they would help bury their father she would divide the land among them. No one would help. She had to bury her father and pay all the taxes for many years before I came along.

I met Lillie Mae daughter and we got married in 1995. Lillie Mae was still in need of money. She sold her daughter (Rose) and me the property Joe Jordan wife posses.

Before I purchase this property, I went to the courthouse and search for the deed for this particular property. The deed description that Joe Jordan gave his wife was 210' x 210'. The property I purchase had a different description.

The agent at the courthouse told me the deed to Elizabeth Jordan does not exist anymore. He stated the description on the deed must fit the property.

Therefore, Rose and I were satisfied with the sale of this property.

Four years later Rose wanted me to buy her share of this property. I purchase her share and a quitclaim deed was issue to me. When this happen the other part of the family wants to take the property from me. They states Lillie Mae should not have sold their mother's property.

I been here ten years and build this property in something. The property that I purchase is on part of the existence property Joe Jordan wife once had.

I would like to know if there is any help for me. As long as their granddaughter name was on the deed, it was not a problem. When they found out, she no longer had it, they wants to take the land back.

I paid for all the land and I had to pay Rose her share. They should have said something in the beginning.

It should be a law against this type of action.

I live in Georgia. Please help with some answers if you can.

Helpless,

Ralph L. Watts

ralphwatts@comcast.net

I did not get any answers or responses.

Here I got a sense that Robert Jordan knew he could loose if we go to court.

He got his sister to call me and ask if I wanted to sell my property.

Below is the letter I sent to my attorney March 31, 2006

Friday, March 31, 2006

J. Baker McGee, Jr.
313 Albany Avenue
P.O. Drawer 679
Waycross, GA 31502-0679

Dear Mr. Baker,
                 RE: Robert J. Jordan vs. Ralph L. Watts

I have no place to live but here in my house. I cannot afford to go anywhere else. I have to take my chances with a jury. All the people heard of this story tells me the jury should be sympathetic when they hear all the facts. I only hope they are right.

Therefore, I am asking if you would go all out to save my property. I believe Robert and his Attorney feel they stand a good chance of losing. That is the reason why they push Robert and his sister to ask me to sale. They came to me; I did not ask them as his attorney said. I want to keep my property.

Please if there is anything, I can do to help just let me know. I go to Jennings, Florida a lot. My mother is ninety-four and not doing well. If you need to call me on my cell phone, the number is 904/305-4415; or email ralphwatts@comcast.net.

Sincerely,

Ralph L. Watts

April 30, 2007 I sent my attorney this email:

Dear Mr. Baker,

I have an email address. It is ralphwatts@comcast.net

If there have to be a meeting, please let me know a couple of days in advance.

Thank you,

Ralph L. Watts

On our next court date my attorney did not show. When court was nearly over he came in the courtroom.

He then went over to Robert's attorney and they went into a vacant room behind the Judge seat. They stayed for a while and Robert's attorneys came out and ask me to go back and talk to my attorney.

I went in to talk with my attorney. The first thing he said was "We got to settle this case". I did not know what he was talking about and then it came; He said "Why don't you pay Robert $5,000.00 and this case will be settled".

I was shocked. He went on "That is the best thing for you and you can keep your property". I looked at him and I almost lost it. I thank God and the prayers my forefathers done for me.

My children told me this was going to happen. Why should I do this?

I sit and thought; well if I get Elizabeth Jordan deed my front property will be 210 feet instead of 85 feet. I told him if I get Elizabeth Jordan deed I will give him the money. "Settle" he said. I went back to my seat. Robert's attorney went back into the room.

Before I can get into my house they were celebrating across the street. And then it came to me the attorneys could lie and I be left in the cold.

Therefore I decided to wait and see if I will get Elizabeth Jordan acre. If I get a deed to her acre and pay $5,000.00 more maybe they would leave me alone.

I really thought that we had to meet with Judge Stephen Jackson to get his approval to resolve this case.

Honorable Judge Stephen L. Jackson had said this case was going to a Jury.

And if it didn't its supposed to be explained before him why? And what was the decision?

I was still waiting to find out when we go before the Judge.

I was going to take my children advice to change my attorney. Therefore when we go before Judge Jackson I will ask to exchange my attorney.

I ask a group of attorneys how I discharge an attorney.

Here is one good answer

November 3 2008 at 5:50 PM (1 minute and 45 seconds later)

What should I do?

Answer

Call the clerk to the judge assigned and ask that the next appearance be moved as you want to discharge your attorney. The court will need to consent. You can ask for a conference for this purpose or raise it if there is a court appearance coming up. Please accept my answer.

I do know and had in mind when we go before Judge Stephen I was going to replace my attorney.

On November 8, 2008 I wrote the Civil Court Clerk the letter below hoping to get the case moved back or delayed.

November 8, 2008

RE: *Jordan vs. Watts*

Civil Action No. 05V-0228

Civil Court

100 South Third Street

Folkston, GA 31537

Dear Clerk of Civil Court,

I am Ralph L. Watts. First, I want to apologize to the Court for what about to take place.

There are some problems with this case. I am 71 years old. When my children found out I was involved, checked and found out the way this case is going they were furious. They thought that since I graduated from the Georgia Police Academy in Forsyth in 12/1989 things like this do not happen. They came a little short of saying I am senile.

I am asking the Court if they would move this case to a later date. I want to discharge my Attorney.

I will or my new Attorney will notify the Court for continuances.

Again, I want to apologize and sincerely hope you can help me in this urgent matter.

Thank you,

Ralph L. Watts

110

I did not get a response from the Court. This really frightened me.

Why I could not get an answer from the Court? Is it because who I am? Then things began to add up. If I lived uptown I would sure get an answer.

Everyone I spoke with could not believe I did not get an answer from the Court. The Courts supposed to be one of the most orderly organizations in existence. Still I received no answer.

All I have got was lots of frustrations and no help or answers.

November 10. 2008 I went online to an attorney searching for answers. I need to fire this attorney.

Below are some answers I received:

November 11, 2008 @ 2:09 am

Replace a Lawyer

Lawyers.com > Find a Lawyer > How to Fire Your Attorney Help Email Page

How to Fire Your Attorney

Lawyers.comsm

No matter how hard we try, some relationships inevitably fail. This doesn't just happen in personal relationships; sometimes your professional relationships can also fall apart. The doctor you initially appreciated because of his efficiency now strikes you as cold and brusque. The hairdresser who you loved in the 1980s doesn't understand that you want a more current style. And the lawyer who you thought would be perfect for your case is now recommending a strategy that you disagree with. It's easy to stop seeing your doctor or hairdresser, but how do you go about firing your attorney while he's in the midst of representing you?

Why Fire Your Attorney?

As a client, you have the right to hire or fire attorneys at will.* But before you fire your attorney, you should give careful thought to your reasons for doing so, other possible solution and the possible ramifications.

Before taking any action, ask yourself these questions:

Am I upset with my attorney because of something he has specifically done, or will the same problem exist with another attorney? For example, if you're upset because of a court ruling, you need to careful consider whether another attorney reasonably could have gotten a different result. If you're asking your attorney to do something that is clearly illegal and your attorney has refused, you will encounter the same situation with a new attorney.

Will changing lawyers be detrimental to my case or legal issue? The courts don't look kindly on people who change lawyers repeatedly. Changing lawyers once in a case is disruptive, but understandable. However if you're lawyer hopping (sometimes call lawyer shopping), it can be seen as an attempt to game the system.

Why am I unhappy with my lawyer's performance?

Some legitimate reasons to consider firing your attorney include that the attorney isn't professional; the attorney doesn't understand your case; you and the attorney disagree about how the case should be handled; you feel as if the attorney is detrimental to the case; or your attorney doesn't show dedication toward your case or compassion toward you as a client.

If, upon reflection, you think you have a valid beef with your attorney, first talk to him about the problem. Lawyers depend on their legal fees to earn a living, so most attorneys are motivated to do a good job and make their clients happy. It can cost you time and money to replace your attorney, so before doing so, explain why you're dissatisfied, and what the attorney would have to do to make you happy as a customer. If you're still dissatisfied after having that conversation, then consider changing attorneys.

Steps to Take

Once you've definitely decided to change attorneys, there are still a few things you should do before notifying him of the change.

Review the written agreement or contract you might have with the attorney. Does it address the steps to be taken to terminate the relationship? You'll want to understand the parameters of that contract as you go about changing lawyers. Your new attorney may also want to see a copy of that agreement.

Also, hire a new attorney. This minimizes the delay in switching attorneys, and also ensures that you're able find good legal representation before firing your existing lawyer. Ask your new attorney whether he will take responsibility for getting your files from your old attorney, or if you should handle that. If you are a party to litigation, confirm that your new lawyer will notify the court as to your change in representation.

Are you're ready to sever the relationship with your old lawyer?

Send a certified or registered letter that clearly states you are terminating the relationship, and that the lawyer is to cease working on any pending matters. Don't get into details about why you're firing him - it's not relevant. In the letter, you request all of your files (or if your new attorney is handling the transfer of files, ask him to cooperate with your new lawyer in this respect). Set a deadline for handing over the files, and detail how you want to receive them. Will you pick them up? Should the attorney send them to you?

If any fees were paid in advance and the work hasn't been done, ask for a refund of the fees. Also, ask for an itemized bill listing all pending fees and expenses. If yours is a contingency case, your new attorney will pay your old attorney from any money that you recover.

The process of changing attorneys can be stressful, but if you maintain a professional demeanor while dealing with your old attorney, it should make things go much more smoothly.

*The possible exception would be in cases where a legal guardian has been appointed to represent a person's best interests because the person is unable to do so himself. In that case, the individual cannot necessarily fire an attorney without the cooperation of the guardian.

Another Response

November 11, 2008 @ 2:26 am

Firing your attorney

What if I have a problem with my attorney?

Firing your attorney - If you aren't happy with the way the attorney you've hired is handling your case, you have the right to dismiss him or her and find another attorney.

Firing an attorney is however, the last step and starting from scratch with another attorney will almost certainly cost you time and therefore, more fees.

Many times, a client's problem with an attorney is a communications problem. You should always let your attorney know of your displeasure and see if a solution can be reached before firing the attorney or making any formal complaint.

Keep in mind that if you do fire an attorney, you will probably be responsible for paying for time and costs associated with your case to that point, so it's not a step to be taken lightly.

That's also why it's important to read and understand any fee for services agreement that you may have signed with an attorney to understand what your financial responsibilities are if you decide to take your case elsewhere.

Once your case has progressed to the point where the attorney has appeared in court on your behalf, a judge will often have to approve a decision to take an attorney off a case.

If you feel an attorney has not acted properly or ethically in your case, you have the right to file a complaint against that attorney with the state bar association.

Again, try to resolve this situation with the attorney before going to this extreme. Once a complaint is filed, it puts you at permanent odds with the attorney and personalities can get in the way of a reasonable resolve of the issue.

If you feel that an attorney has billed you improperly for services performed or has failed to refund an unearned portion of an advance payment, you may request that the dispute be submitted to arbitration. Most Bar associations maintain a statewide fee arbitration program or similar such program to assist in resolving fee disputes without the necessity of litigation.

This is another answer:

Mad at Your Lawyer?:

You have a gripe: you've hired a lawyer to take care of your interests and now realize that he/she is doing a lousy job. Maybe he isn't working on your case, settled without your authorization, overcharged. Maybe she was irresponsible, improperly dropping your case or providing incompetent services.

Can I break up and fire my attorney?

Yes. If you are having trouble, are unhappy and it can't be worked out, you can fire your lawyer, for any reason (if your case is in active litigation, the judge's approval may have to be obtained). Do it in writing and request that your files be returned to you. Be prepared to lose any retainer you may have already paid.

Before pulling the plug and hiring a replacement, consider the following:

(1) The attorney that you fired is entitled to be paid for work already done. If you have been paying your attorney all along, and you are current, this may not be a problem. However, if your lawyer has taken your case on a contingency fee basis, the attorney is entitled to payment for the time spent on your case, plus any costs and expenses. If you have not paid your bill, your ex-lawyer can sue you for unpaid fees. Firing does not mean you don't have to pay a bill that you have already run up.

117

(2) If you hire, you may be starting from scratch, as the replacement will have to get up to speed on your case, which may be an additional cost.

Can my lawyer drop me as a client?

Yes, but not because he or she is not making money, or because a better, more lucrative case just walked into his or her door, or because the matter is taking longer than anticipated. If your case is in active litigation, the lawyer can't just hightail it out without the judge's authorization.

Some of the most common reasons the lawyer will drop a case include:

conflict of interest;

nonpayment of legal services already rendered;

client-lawyer communication: the client does not keep his or her end of the bargain.

I'm being gouged--Sticker shock syndrome.

By far the top complaint of clients about their attorneys has to do with attorney fees. Speak up! Ask for an explanation of the charge; be businesslike and straightforward. Errors, misunderstandings, and adjustments agreeable to both parties can be made. If there is a stalemate, read your written agreement; many require that fee disputes be resolved through arbitration.

The lawyer is not talking, at least not to you.

You're the boss. The frequency of the contact and the form it takes will vary according to your case. Unnecessary calls (e.g., lawyer has no news to report) are costly, if you're being billed at an hourly rate. A good way to deal with this is to write a detailed letter, explaining your disappointment, outrage, and the need for good communication. Another solution would be to ask for a written status report on some weekly or monthly basis, regardless of whether there is anything new in your case.

If the lawyer persistently ignores your phone calls, it may be time to re-evaluate the relationship. Act quickly if you decide to pursue this course of action since you want to make sure the transition is smooth.

The attorney has done next to nothing on my behalf.

Keep in mind that lawsuits move very slowly and it is not uncommon for heaps of time to pass.

That said, you have every right to be kept up-to-date on the progress and status of your case. Just how closely you need to be kept informed should be discussed up-front.

A good way to deal with this is to type a letter, keep it concise, businesslike, and to the point. But let the attorney know that that you are not pleased, that you are not being treated the way you want, and you are disappointed. Ask for a face-to-face meeting (if possible) to air your grievance and at that meeting or phone conversation, ask what has been done and what will be done.

If you still cannot resolve the matter, contact your state bar association; they will examine the charges. However, before

you proceed with this course of action, be sure you have lined up a replacement attorney.

Attorney not on the up-and-up: Dealing with ethics issues.

It happens. An attorney takes money from a client and never does a lick of work. An attorney bribes a juror; an attorney botches the legal work; an attorney files false papers; an attorney abandons the client. And so on, and so forth. Not all lawyers are crooks, despite the stereotype that the legal profession is infested by a thriving cult of greed and power. The vast majority of lawyers lead straightforward, conventional lives, and maintain high ethical standards.

If you feel that your attorney has in some way been unscrupulous, speak up; try to resolve the matter amicably between you. It may well be that the problem is only a failure of communication. Or get in touch with the state bar association who will advise you on how to file a grievance. The association policies its members and will investigate complaints and, if valid, will institute disciplinary action against the attorney.

My "good" attorney confided in his buddy (my cousin) some information about my case. Is that a breach of ethics?

Yes. If the attorney disclosed confidential information to his buddy concerning your case, it is a violation of his or her duty and a violation of the rules of ethics. He can be disbarred (i.e. his license to practice law can be taken away from him).

Here is an answer for me to do:

Should I sue my lawyer for malpractice?

In law, as in every profession, there are always practitioners whose methods and conduct are subject to criticism. In law, malpractice means that the attorney, through error or omission, fails to use the same degree of care, skill, and judgment as other lawyers practicing in your community. This does not mean you can sue if another attorney beats your lawyer, or your lawyer has achieved dismal results, or is arrogant, volatile and blustery, cynical or intractable, or doesn't return your calls. You can sue only if he or she renders work or assistance of minimal competence and you are damaged as a result. You can sue where there is a breach of ethics (e.g., a conflict of interest) or civil fraud (recovered money but didn't pay it over).

Filing an attorney malpractice suit differs from filing a grievance with the bar association. Among other requirements, a lawsuit requires proof and, if successful, the winner gets damages. Such cases are highly contested, strongly defended, and very expensive.

 Another answer:

Firing Your Lawyer First off, before you give up on your lawyer altogether, try writing him a letter, explaining the problems you're having with him. A formal communication of this sort may get his attention. Bear in mind that clients and lawyers frequently get frustrated with each other right before and during trial (when both client and lawyer are anxious and irritable)—and this type of friction can often be worked out.

When it does become necessary, it's pretty easy to dump your lawyer. You can just say: "You're fired," or words to that effect. However, if your lawyer has come to court on your behalf and "made a general appearance" (gone on record as your lawyer), then she has to get the judge's permission to withdraw from your case. And the judge will want whoever's taking over to "substitute in as the new attorney of record."

If you're just switching from one private attorney to a different private attorney, the lawyers themselves will handle the paperwork.

If you're firing your attorney and planning to represent yourself, then the judge has to hold a Faretta hearing to decide whether you're competent to do so (see Representing Yourself).

If you've got a public defender that you don't like, it can be difficult to get a different court-appointed lawyer. First, you should try talking to your attorney's supervisor about it. Even if you're not given a new lawyer, the one you've got may work harder, knowing that the supervisor is paying attention. If this is not satisfactory, you can ask the judge to appoint a different attorney, but judges are reluctant to do so, particularly if you're close to trial. You may have to convince the judge that your public defender has behaved really inappropriately or else completely ignored you, and there's no way you can work together effectively. It will help if you keep a list of your lawyer's offensive or inadequate actions and statements, and write letters to your lawyer describing the problem you're having with him (keep copies, of course).

If you change lawyers, it will almost always delay your case.

The new lawyer will want to ask the judge for a continuance (extension), in order to digest all the information in the case and undertake tasks that the old lawyer didn't do.

If you fire a privately retained lawyer, you don't necessarily get any of your money back. Most fee agreements state that the fee is non-refundable. If you're parting from your lawyer on reasonably friendly terms and she hasn't done much work yet, you may be able to negotiate a partial refund—but don't count on it.

If you've fired your lawyer, he's required to give a copy of the file he created for your case to the new lawyer (or to you, if you're representing yourself). It's illegal for an attorney to hold the file hostage, even if you owe him money.

I think I have enough information to act. This attorney didn't do anything to help me. It is a shame to have someone in a court home claiming to be an attorney and the Courts let him get away with this.

Every attorney should be held responsible for a high rating on representation.

Monday, November 24, 2008

McGee and McGee, PC

313 Albany Avenue

Waycross, GA 31502-0679

Re: Jordan vs. Watts

Civil Action No. 05V-0228

Dear Mr. McGee,

I am writing this letter to let you know I am terminating our Client /Attorney relationship. The reasons listed below.

1. On our first court date, the Judge recommended this case go to a Jury. (Instead, you wanted to settle out of court.)
2. I have the feeling you do not understand my case. (I want you to speak with the one person to clear everything up/you did not)
3. You do not show dedication toward my case or compassion to me as a client.

4. I ask you to send me an explanation for my fees or an itemized bill. (You refused).

There is nothing much left but to ask for dismissal of the entire Legal Documents agreeable beforehand

I hope this can continue in a professional manner. I understand my rights as a client and I believe you did not serve in my best interest.

As of this date, please cease working on any pending matters.

I need my files and remaining money that belong to me.

Please send an itemized bill of fees charged and all pending fees expenses.

Thank you,

Ralph L. Watts

I waited for a response from Mr. McGee but I was very disappointed. He refused to send anything. This is unprofessional as you can get.

This is the law:

If you've fired your lawyer, he's required to give a copy of the file he created for your case to the new lawyer (or to you,

 if you're representing yourself). **It's illegal for an attorney to hold the file hostage, even if you owe him money**.

This guy broke all the laws and the Courts and Georgia Bar Association agrees with this type of action. (Pitiful; Huh?)

This is very unprofessional and you will see at the end the Georgia Bar Association agreed with everything he done. Yeah, this is Georgia.

Absolutely Nothing: But took my money

120

The attorney I had did absolutely nothing. I ask him to investigate and take a statement from Willie V. Harvey. Willie V. Harvey knew Robert Jordan was a drunk during the years in question.

He lies when he said he built his mother's house also he lied stating I knew about his family before I came to Folkston, Georgia in 1994. These lies should be dealt with; this is a Court of Law and they are notarized on record and recorded in the Court records. This is perjury and should not be allowed.

The worst part of this he told The Georgia Bar Association that this was decided in an open Court. That is the biggest lie he can tell. He should be heavily fined for lying.

On the second day we suppose to meet he was late. When he did get there he and Robert's attorney went in a back room in the Courthouse. They devised their little scheme and it worked.

My attorney calls me in a back room and that is where I got the bad news about paying off Robert. I did not have time to think or seek answers. I had to tell him now.

Therefore I told him I will give Robert $5,000.00 for **Elizabeth Jordan acre.** I did not get the deed to Elizabeth Jordan acre. I got a phony deed to Lillie Mae Harvey property.

What I got was not what I asked for. I really didn't get anything.

I know it got to be against the law to sign and give a phony deed to someone. The deed I got is phony because Elizabeth Jordan had a 210x210.

The law said no one can change the name or measurements on the deed. This is what Robert Jordan and his attorney schemed up. If I did this they would put me in jail.

Ones that know the law and break it should pay double the price.

December 10, 2008 I went by Attorney Robert W. Guy in Kingsland, Georgia.

I ask him a few questions and they were the best answers I heard in two years.

Later I wrote him this letter:

Friday, December 12, 2008

Robert W. Guy Jr, Atty.

52 Camden Woods Pkwy

Kingsland, Georgia 31558

Mr. Guy,

Thanks for the information you provided for me Wednesday. That was more info than my Attorney gave all year.

I have something else I would appreciate if you can do this for me. Around June of this year a 100 share Certificate No. 0563 from the First National Corp was cash or traded. The name on that Certificate is mind. (Ralph Watts) Would you find out the total value of these shares?

I know you are an expensive Attorney and I would like to pay you in multiple payments.

If you can help me in this situation, I sure would appreciate it.

Thank you,

Ralph L. Watts

Ralph L. Watts

5813 Rover Drive

Jacksonville, FL 32244

December 12, 2008 I wrote the Probate Judge Honorable Phillips:

Friday, December 12, 2008

RE; Jordan *vs*. Watts

Civil Action No. 05V-0228

The Honorable Judge Phillips

100 South Third Street

Folkston, GA 31537

Dear Judge Phillips;

 I went to Kingsland and spoke with Attorney Robert Guy Wednesday, December 10, 2008. I got more information from him in a few minutes than my original Attorney in the whole year.

My problem was when I received the order from the court it scared me to death. I rushed out in a hurry and got an Attorney. I did not have time to make a good selection. Never the less I made this choice and I do believe my Attorney actions were not in my best interest.

The property Robert is suing me for belong to someone else. The people next door are the ones who lives on seventy-five (75%) of the property in this case. This is the reason I believe Robert's Attorney did not want a jury trail. He persuaded my Attorney to get me to pay Robert then all is good.

I spoke with a person with the Bar Association. What I can get from our conservation is if I am telling the truth this whole case could be reverse. There were no promising made but my outlook seems better.

Since my Attorney is uncooperative I will continue make these payments to Robert's Attorney.

I want to thank you for your cooperation in this urgent situation.

Thankfully,

Ralph L. Watts

I could not get any good information from the attorney

> Re: *Jordan vs. Watts*

> Civil Action No. 05V-0228

Dear Mr. Bacon,

There have been some problems and I am hoping you and I can resolve them.

First in the emails I sent my Attorney in May and June (email enclosed), I ask him to change the payment date from the 15th to the 25th. This he did not do.

Second, I ask him some personal information involving client/attorney relationship. He refused to give me this information. I had to excuse him from our relationship. (Letter enclosed).

I am asking you if you would agree the payments date be change to the 25th. If you will agree to this please let me know.

In this letter are payments for November and December 2008. The remaining payments I will send to you (If you agree) by the 25th.

I read your book "Miracle in Michigan". A great book everyone should read. I wrote one some twenty years ago. "The Futurity Race" I classified it as a Religious Fiction because I did not use the correct people name.

Please let me hear from you about receiving and changing payment dates.

I thank you very much for your cooperation in this urgent matter.

Godly grateful,

Ralph L. Watts

I really thought this guy was an alright Christian. I read his book and he told a very good Christian story.

I received this letter from him dated December 31, 2008:

125

Bacon Law Firm, P.C.

Post Office Box 5880
St. Marys, Georgia 31558

Gary A. Bacon, Attorney

Telephone 912 882-7322
Facsimile 912-882-8017

87 B Hawthorne Lane

Email: gbacon@baconlawfirm.com
Website: baconlawfirm.com

December 31, 2008

Mr. Ralph Watts
PO Box 36
Folkston, GA 31537

Dear Mr. Watts:

Mr. Jordan has agreed to allow you to continue to pay on the 25th of the month without any additional late fees, provided that you will agree to what is written in the promissory note to pay said payments directly to him at his address Route 2 Box 4098, Folkston, Georgia 31537. This would allow him to get the payments more quickly.

I appreciate your kind comments about my book. I am glad that you had the opportunity to read it.

If you have an extra copy of your book, please send it to me so that I may read it in the future as well.

Also, enclosed is a copy of the note and amortization schedule that shows exactly how much interest you would be paid for tax purposes.

Your cooperation in getting this matter resolved is most appreciated.

With kind personal regards, I remain,

Sincerely,

Bacon Law Firm, P.C.

Gary A. Bacon

Enclosures
GAB/rmd

This is part of the lie McGee sent to the Georgia Bar Association:

When you read Rule 1.16 he wrote "the conclusion with the settlement he had accepted and approved in open court".

The Georgia Bar accepted this lie. This is the reason why I said they did not investigate this claim. If they would have they would have found out their open court is a back room with the door close.

127

McGEE AND McGEE, P.C.

ATTORNEYS AT LAW
313 ALBANY AVENUE
P.O. DRAWER 679
WAYCROSS, GEORGIA 31502-0679

J. BAKER McGEE, JR.
JAMES BAKER McGEE, III

February 17, 2009

TELEPHON
912-285-03:
FAX
912-285-47:

EXHIBIT "B"

State Bar of Georgia
Office of General Counsel
104 Marietta Street, Suite 100
Atlanta, Georgia 30303

Re: Grievance of Ralph Watts

Dear Sirs:

You indicated that this grievance may involve these rules and I will respond to each of them separately.

Rule 1.14 - Client Under Disability.

I have no reason to think that Mr. Watts is mentally or physically disabled. All of my contacts with him were normal. He always appeared to understand any conversation. In reviewing the documents sent by you, I am still not sure what, if any, disability is supposed to exist.

Rule 1.115 (II) – Record Keeping Trust Accounts.

At no time did I have any money belonging to Mr. Watts which would go into my Trust Account, except when I was paid. The way I was paid was that some stock was sold and the proceeds split. That money was deposited and disbursed on the day it was received with my fee coming to me and the balance being paid to Mr. Watts. After his case was settled he sent to me checks payable to the Plaintiff pursuant to the settlement. I held those checks in my file pending receipt of Mr. Watts deed following approval from the probate court. When the deed was received I forwarded these uncashed checks to the Plaintiff's attorney who presumably negotiated them. Copies of 2 checks are enclosed.

Rule 1.16 – Declining or Withdrawing From Representation.

I neither declined nor withdrew from representation of Mr. Watts. Sometime after the case was settled, Mr. Watts began to find fault with the settlement, Mr. Watts wrote me that he did not wish for me to represent him. At that point the case was over and there was no representation left. I took the case when he hired me and represented him until its conclusion with the settlement he had accepted and approved in open court. Although, I did not bill him any more, I continued to help him by holding the checks to the Plaintiff while awaiting the deed from the Plaintiff. My response to his

128

I was really upset at the fee I was charged therefore; on February 24,
2009 I wrote this letter to the Georgia Bar asking for help.

5813 Rover Drive
Jacksonville, FL 32244
RE: Jordan vs. Watts/Civil Action 05V-0228

State Bar of Georgia
104 Marietta Street, Suite 100
Atlanta, Georgia 30303

Dear Ms. Payne,

I will try to explain in this letter what happen.

I received a Civil Court order. So afraid I rushed out and got the first Attorney I
could find.

I did not have any money. I did have a Certificate in my bank deposit box. This
Certificate was 100 shares of First National Bank stock. (My retirement money)

I signed this Certificate over to him to hold for my fee. The values suppose to be
$9100.00.

At the first court date, he was there and the Judge recommended this case go
before a Jury.

Both Attorneys agreed and I was very happy with this. I knew we could win this
case because this whole case was full of lies.

129

At the second court date, my Attorney was late. My Attorney and the other Attorney had a meeting in a back room. After they met, my Attorney called me in. He said to me "We got to settle this case. I want you to pay Robert $5,000.00 and he will give you a clear deed" I was shocked out of my skin. He acted as if he turned against me. Now I was in a trap. He also stated I should make a large payment down to show good faith.

He took unto himself to fill out how I should pay this $5,000.00. In addition, the kicker I had to send the money to him before it was agree in court.

The main thing when he cashes my Certificate, he took more than half of my money.

I only got $3500.00 back. He said the Certificate was $7400.00, which is $2000.00 less than the value the shares were worth.

I learned that the other Attorney was paid $900.00. The other Attorney did all the work putting this case together.

I delivered all the certified copies to his office. He did not make one trip to Folkston for any certified copies. I fell he is due less than the other Attorney. $800.00 is the most he is entitle to. $2,700.00 should be return to me.

Ralph L. Watts

I sent this letter March 10, 2009 to the Grievance Counsel at The State Bar

130

Tuesday, March 10, 2009

State Bar of Georgia

Office of General Counsel

104 Marietta Street, Suite 100

Atlanta, Georgia 30303

Dear Grievance Counsel,

I totally disagree with Mr. McGee Fee invoice.

That is the reason he never would give an itemize copy of the charges he sent you. He did not spend 12 hours on the total case. He said he spent 1.5 hours in Probate Court. The first date of court he did argue the case. That took less than ten (10) minutes because the Judge asks them to take this before a Jury. Both Attorneys agreed.

The next court date we were, suppose to be assign a date for court to begin. He was late coming to court. He missed the calling; this is when Mr. McGee and Mr. Bacon (other attorney) went in a room behind the Judge chair.

In this room, they made the decision to make me pay. There was no pre-trial consolidation or initial conference. These fees had to be made up to fit what I am being charged. I had about five no more than six office visits. They all were less than 15 minutes. I did spend about twenty minutes on one. His son went to the bank with me to notarize cashing the certificate.

I know this is unusual but I beg you, please check this story out. Mr. Bacon seems to be an honorable man. Please talk with him. Mr. Bacon put twice the time in this case as Mr. McGee. All the families (children, grandchildren and great grandchildren) had to sign papers for this to take place. I do not believe Mr. Bacon hours or fees are like the one I am being charged. Please, I know this is probably not part of you job. Just this once please speaks with Mr. Bacon. I believe he will tell the truth.

I sincerely thank for all your cooperation in this urgent matter.

Ralph L. Watts

5813 Rover Drive

Jacksonville, FL 32244

Gary A. Bacon, Attorney/Tele-912 882-7322/email:gbacon@baconlawfirm.com

I wrote this letter March 11, 2009

Wednesday, March 11, 2009

State Bar of Georgia

Office of General Counsel

104 Marietta Street, Suite 100

Atlanta, Georgia 30303

Re: J. B. McGee

Dear General Counsel

I forgot to mention Judge Phillips. If you speak with Judge Phillips, I am sure he will tell this case was handle in an unusual way. Judge Phillips is the Probate Judge.

I believe on the second court date (He was late) the agreement made sent by mail to Judge Phillips to sign off on it. Judge Phillips will tell you this case went in an unusual way.

Judge Phillips number is 912 496-2230.

Thank you,

Ralph L. Watts

I am still searching for answers. April 7, 2009 I asked another group of attorneys these questions:

Tuesday, April 07, 2009

Thanks for the chance to assist

Question one: When a deed is made up or out; is the description on the deed supposes to match the property? This I mean match or tells you what and where your property is located.

Yes...that is the purpose of a deed...to describe with specificity the property to which it relates.

Question two: How important is the description on a deed?

<u>Well, it must describe the property to be effective</u>. So, if for example, there is a home in San Diego, CA that a person wants to sell, and the deed transfers "123 4th street, San Diego, CA". So long as there is only 1 property with that address, it would be valid. But if, for example the deeds said "my 4th street house" this would not likely be effective (or a valid transfer)

Question three: **How may one change a deed description? And by what authority?**

<u>Only the maker can, and typically only prior to transfer</u>.

Question four: Can a person who does not have the authority to sell a deed property, change the description on this deed?

No, <u>see above</u>

Thank you guys,

Ralph L. Watts

Please let me know if you have further questions; if so I will do my best to answer them. If not please hit the accept button, its the only way I get credit for my work.

On September 09, 2009 I sent these questions and answers to Honorable Judge Phillips.

I want everyone to know by law no one suppose to change the maker of Elizabeth Jordan deed.

It should be a 210 sq acre.

Robert Jordan and his attorney changed the inserts of the original Elizabeth Jordan deed.

Wednesday, September 09, 2009

Civil Action 05V-228

Honorable Robert F. Phillips, Judge

Charlton Probate Court

100 South Third Street

Folkston, Georgia 31537

Dear Honorable Phillips,

I was very angry the way this Civil Action took place, therefore I took this case to three Law Firms. I needed some answers because I believe something was wrong.

135

Each Firm agrees the way this Action went is not proper. They also come short of saying my Attorney was working for the Plaintiff.

They do agree that Lillie Mae Harvey should not have sign the deed for her mother.

They also agree that Robert Jordan have the right be Administrator of Elizabeth Jordan property only.

They disagree that Robert Jordan can be Administrator of property that Lillie Mae Harvey had a right to sell me. That property was not owned by Elizabeth Jordan and should not be mention in this Action.

They disagree that an Administrator cannot change the description on a document. (i.e.) Robert Jordan wants to use Elizabeth Jordan deed to become Administrator and then change the deed to other property. This they say he cannot use the property I rightfully owned for Elizabeth Jordan property..

One thing they made stand out. The deed I am entitled to is the deed that Joe Jordan gave to his wife. They told me to make sure the descriptions are the same. (Word for word)

They told me you have the power to set things straight. If by some reason I cannot get the original deed please let me know. I want to have time selecting the right Attorney.

I do thank you for your cooperation in this urgent matter.

Gratefully,

Ralph L. Watts

I did not get ant responses; still again I am lost hoping to get things right.

It is very hard to live in this world around a lot of sinful people.

It is also hard when people in charge are sinful and you get involve with them in any situation.

I found myself there and without God no one can survive.

I found myself back at Krystal on Lem Turner in Jacksonville.

I told the guys all what I am involve in and the trouble its causing me.

All the guys tell me to get out and do not try to fight. Even if you are right you cannot win. You will get killed. Someway or somehow they will get rid of you.

As I listen to them brings the horror I seen at my hometown years ago. I say to myself be it possible in time to see ugly things again?

I had to leave; I told them I appreciate what they have said and it possible to happen again.

I came back to Folkston still looking for answers.

I received this letter From Honorable Judge Phillips:

He knew that order he signed was not Elizabeth Jordan acre of land.

I paid Robert Jordan $5000.00 for Elizabeth Jordan acre. That acre is a 210x210. The law is only the maker can change the name on the deed. What I got from Robert Jordan and his attorney is a phony deed.

I received this letter from the Probate Judge. He stated he did not say which property Elizabeth Jordan. Does he have to say? She only had one piece of property. She only own one property which Robert Jordan used to get me into court.

The law said you cannot switch properties or change the names. This is what they did and the Probate Judge knew this..

The problem here is they taken all my money and an attorney would

Charlton County, Georgia

PROBATE COURT

BOB PHILLIPS, Judge
SHEILA B. WOOLARD, Clerk
100 South Third Street • Folkston, Georgia 31537 • (912) 496-2230

September 28, 2009

Mr. Ralph Watts:

The Charlton Probate Court received your letter regarding Civil Action 05V-228, handled in Charlton Superior Court. I have a copy of the agreement that you signed to pay money to the estate of Elizabeth Jordan.

When I signed the order in Probate Court appointing Robert Jordan as Administrator of the Estate of Elizabeth Jordan that was not saying what property Elizabeth Jordan owned at the time of her death.

Your relief will be in Superior Court.

Robert F. Phillips, Probate Judge
Charlton County, Georgia

139

not take this case. Once again I am shut off from receiving justice.

I wrote this letter to The Georgia State Bar asking for help.

Sunday, November 01, 2009

Ralph L. Watts

5813 Rover Drive

Jacksonville, Florida 32244

State Bar of Georgia

104 Marietta Street, Suite 100

Atlanta, Georgia 30303

c/o Rita Payne, Director/Fee Arbitration

RE: Fee Dispute with James Baker McGee III

Dear Ms. Payne:

Thank you once again for your help and advisement.

In the beginning things were happening so fast I was just doing

140

what ever I could to try and survived. The only thing I remember about Item number 5 on the Fee Arbitration application is after I met in Judge Phillips office a few weeks later I received an order to come to court. Then I rushed out for an Attorney.

About item #6 this had to be the first part of 2008. (Possible March) I am not sure. I was sure we would go back for a hearing which did not take place.

I enclose a few items and maybe this will help you make a resolution of what went on.

In the beginning things were not good for me. I enclosed a letter written to Ann Rewis in 2005.

Item#1 this was the first meeting we had in Judge Phillips office. The Court Reporter was ordered by the opposing Attorney (which I did not know about) but it was stated we would share her cost of $90.00. I had to pay the whole bill under protest.

Item#2 A letter saying to my Attorney a trail is necessary.

Item#3 A loan schedules made out ahead of time to hurry and settle this case.

Item#4 A letter from my Attorney asking me to come in and sign some papers.

Item#5 A letter to my Attorney (McGee) questioning the validity of the fee I was being charged.

Item#6 A letter from my Attorney justifying the fees without a trial.

Item#7 A letter to my Attorney hoping he would reconsider the fee he had charged.

Item#8 A letter to the Court outlining I would reject this offer when I get in Court.

Item#9 A letter to Judge Phillips outlining the coercing the Attorneys had convincing me to go along with them.

Item#10 A letter to the opposing Attorney outlining the problems and mistakes my Attorney has made. (Ask him for help)

Item#11 A letter from the opposing Attorney with a good answer.

Item#12 A letter to Judge Phillips explaining the problems I should not have had in the first place with an Attorney working for me.

 This is what I have to show with a working Attorney I would not have these problems. As one Attorney put it; "This case is easy, all you have to do is follow the law" The law was not followed in this case and I believe I am entitle to a large refund.

Again I thank you for your help in this case.

Sincerely yours,

Ralph L. Watts

Monday, January 11, 2010

RE: FEE Arbitration & Civil Action NO. 05V-0228

Ms. Rita Payne

State Bar of Georgia

104 Marietta Street NW

Atlanta, GA 30303

Dear Ms. Payne,

I tried my best to solve this matter that should not have taken place. When I asked for most of my Fees returned, I did not want to get anyone in trouble because we all make mistakes.

I have enclosed copies of the problem with this Civil Action. On copy #1 you will see I legally owned the Blue Diagram A, B, C & D. This property should not have been mention in the Civil Action. The property E, F, G & H is the property the Civil Action is about.

I mention this to Judge Phillips and he said he did not make Robert Jordan   Administrator of no other property but the property of Elizabeth Jordan. This is the property E, F, G & H.

Two law firms told me the reason they wanted this settle out of court because the written order that was presented (Civil Action-#05V-0228) is in appropriate. Both Attorneys knew this and they persuaded me to take their advice. They did not want this Action in a Trial.

142

I am really tired of this. There are two Attorneys who have promoted an act against the Court and no one seems to care. They knew better than to present something like this in the first place. That is the reason at the first meeting the Judge asks them to take it to a Jury. This meant trouble and they decided to use me as a guinea pig.

All I asked for is someone to check what happen to see if my Attorney was worth what he was paid. As you can see he did absolutely nothing. As one Attorney put it, this is an easy case. I pay Robert Jordan and get the property I deserves. Not the property I legally own.

The #2 copy you will see at the end they added the property I legally own. A, B, C & D.

Thank you,

Ralph L. Watts

Sunday, May 30, 2010

Gary A. Bacon, Atty.

Post Office Box 5880

St. Marys, Georgia 31558

> Re: *Jordan vs. Watts*

> Civil Action No. 05V-0228

Dear Mr. Bacon,

I am writing because I made overpayment of this case. I am supposed to make 24 payments of $200.00.and one final payment of $97.97. These $200.00 payments began 05/25/08 and end 04/25/10. One final payment of $97.97 was due 05/25/10. On 05/25/10 a payment of $200.00 was paid which is an overpayment of $102.03. Please I would appreciate it very much if your Client issues a refund.

I am also including a copy of Elisabeth Jordan deed. Please when Robert Jordan sign this deed let them read identical.

I do not want anymore problems with this property out here. I want to make sure this acre of land is clear and no one else comes after me.

My health is not to well right now. I am staying around family until I can do better. If you will please send me the Elisabeth Jordan deed to the address below.I planned to get in touch with Rose Harvey (Lillie Mae Harvey's daughter/divorce wife) to see if she wants this property. She is the only family member did not sign against me.

Please help me out on this and your cooperation will be grateful appreciated.incerely,

Ralph L. Watts

CC: Honorable Robert F. Phillips

    File

The next day I went to Jacksonville, Florida.

Back at Krystal I told the guys what was going on with my life in Folkston.

They beg me to do nothing and leave Folkston. They will kill you if you try to expose them or try to get help. They do not want the outside to know what is going on.

Listening to them put fear in my mind. I thought maybe I better seek help.

On the way back to Folkston I realize there is a doubled standard there.

I remember back in 1995 or 1996 I was driving west on main street one block from second street. A guy that owns a business in that vicinity backs his truck in the passenger side of my car.

We called the police to investigate. When the police arrived (Wesley) the investigation began.

Wesley walking around writing information and the guy that caused the accident was in all smiles. I never have seen an accident where the causer was happy.

When the investigation ended the causer did not get a ticket. The guy got in his truck and said "Thank you Wesley" He drove off.

Now what do you think if I had back into his truck? I would have gotten a ticket. Now I am really frightened. Believe me this type of living is no good anywhere.

It's a shame we have communities with so little knowledge to manage on righteous living. It always got to be crooks at the top and if you say or do anything you will be on their black book.

Everywhere you go you will be harassed by police or lose at the shopping desk.

This book is written without the knowledge of ones I believe is involved in corruption activities. I do believe once its out there I will be harassed every day and probably more.

In the meantime I am seeking help.

I chose the law office of Charlena Thorpe and sent an email.

YOUR EMAIL HAS BEEN SENT.

Firm Name: Law Office of Charlena Thorpe, Inc.

(Contact: Charlena Thorpe) Date Sent: 2010-06-16 12:54:47

Your Name: Ralph Watts

Your City: GA

Your Email: ralphwatts@comcast.net

Your Daytime Phone: 904 305-7224

Alternate Phone Number: 904 305-7224

The Question Involves: Myself

Visitor's Question:

Hello,

What I have is unbelievable. I am involved in a Probate Court suit. The Attorneys from both sides have worked together. I believe they had done the unthinkable scam in this land deal.

I had to pay my Attorney $3500.00 for one court appearance. The second time he came to court he was late. I had another firm to look at the court presentation and they said it should not have been accepted by any court.

I have paid an extra $5,000.00 for this acre of land and have not received a deed. I learned he want to issue a deed for another parcel. I am staying quiet.

I want them to do all their ugly stuff. Then I want an Attorney who is not afraid to go against Attorneys or a County. One Law firm told me to make sure this court is not held in that County.

This is huge, if you would like to read this case I will send all for an evaluation. Now I am waiting (month) to see if they send me a deed. One question: After one fulfill the Court's settlements, how long must one wait on a Administrator's Deed? Please let me know.

NOTE:

The remaining letter I cannot find:

147

I am still afraid that something might happen to me I wrote this to jocksmith.com.

karla@jocksmith.com<karla@jocksmith.com>;

Hello Karla,

I am involve in a probate case in a small town in Georgia. This case is like the 1920s or 1940s. African Americans do not have the understanding of law and everything goes in this court of law.

I have been mistreated from the beginning. I had to pay an Attorney $3500.00 to handle a probate case with the value of this acre of land is $2,000.00 not more than $2,500.00. I was told Attorneys are not allowed to charge more than 3 to 7 o/o of the estate value. I had to pay $5,000.00 plus interest for this acre. This total comes near $9,000.00 for one acre of land.

The first kicker my Attorney made one Court appearance. The second Court appearance he was late and made a deal in a back room with the other Attorney to settle this case not in my favor.

The second kicker is they will not issue a deed for this acre. It has been over thirty days after I sent a letter to the Attorney with a cc. to the Probate Judge asking for the deed to this property. They hoping I will die and they will still have the land. I am 73 years old.

148

I have the proof one need to win this case. I just need someone who is not afraid to go against other Attorneys, Judges and this county.

Please let me know if you can help. I can assure this will be a high profile case. I also believe they will settle out of court because what went on is very embarrassing.

I do thank you for your help in this urgent matter.

Very Truly,

Ralph L. Watts

.

Dear Gate City Bar Association,

I am involve in a probate case in a small town in Georgia. This case

is like the 1920s or 1940s. African Americans do not have the

understanding of law and everything goes in this court of law.

I have been mistreated from the beginning. I had to pay an Attorney

$3500.00 to handle a probate case with the value of this acre of land

is $2,000.00 not more than $2,500.00. I was told Attorneys are not allowed to charge more than 3 to 7 o/o of the estate value. I had to pay $5,000.00 plus interest for this acre. This total comes near $9,000.00 for one acre of land.

149

The first kicker my Attorney made one court appearance. The second Court appearance he was late and made a deal in a back room with the other attorney to settle this case not in my favor.

The second kicker is they will not issue a deed for this acre. It has been over thirty days after I sent a letter to the Attorney with a

cc. to the Probate Judge asking for the deed to this property. They hoping I will die and they will still have the land. I am 73 years old.

I have the proof one need to win this case. I just need someone who

is not afraid to go against other Attorneys, Judges and this county.

Please let me know if you can help. I can assure this will be a high profile case. I also believe they will settle out of court because they know they are wrong.

I do thank you for your help in this urgent matter.

Very Truly,

Ralph L. Watts

From: Shukura L. Ingram

To: ralphwatts

Sent: Thursday, June 24, 2010 6:28 PM

Subject: Re: Probate Case

Mr. Watts - we received your email. We are an association made of up attorneys but the Gate City Bar Association does not take on cases.

We can send your request for an attorney out to our lawyers to see if anyone is interested in your case.

Unfortunately, there are no guarantees that someone will take your case. If you send me the county where the property is and your telephone number, we will be happy to send your request out to other lawyers.

~President, Gate City Bar Association

Hello again,

I forgot to mention this. I want to file at least a lawsuit against these people. There is no way I would mention this to a local attorney. I would like for this suit to be filed in Atlanta or

Savannah; not in this county.

I am thinking about moving because I fear for my life. I would like for this to be quiet as possible until I move my stuff out this house.

This is a sure winner. I have all the information needed to win this case.

I just need an Attorney that is not afraid to stand up.

If you know an Attorney in another state who can practice in Georgia would also work. I really hate for this to get away.

I understand you are an Association, but an Association I think would have great relationships with Attorneys. That is what I am looking for.

Please speak with an experience Probate Attorney and if he want some easy money; here it is.

Thanks again,

Ralph L. Watts

From: Shukura L. Ingram

> To: ralphwatts

> Sent: Saturday, June 26, 2010 11:54 AM

> Subject: Re: Fw: Probate Case

> Mr. Watts you'll need to provide me with a phone number and you need to > me the name of the county. Also, lawsuits have to be filed in the county > where the property/estate is.

I am about gone now; I am really losing it; feel helpless with this terrible headache I know my blood pressure is at the ceiling. I pray and ask God to help me through this.

> Mrs. Ingram,

> I thank you. Please do not get me killed. I am truly afraid.

> The counties of Charlton (Folkston), Ware (Waycross) or Camden county are the counties where most all the trouble started.

> Please I would like to have an Attorney who is familiar with> discrimination in cases. > This incident happen in Folkston, GA (Charlton cty).

My phone number is 904-305-7224. I have many ugly calls so please if someone call let them leave me a message.

> Once again I beg you, do not let this get out. I know what can happen to > me.

> Let me tell you this. You probably from a large city and never had this > problem. I was born and raised in Jennings, FL. This is a small town close to Valdosta, GA. Today a black man cannot open a pool room or a store. If the kids there want to play pool they have to go to Jasper, FL or Valdosta, GA. The Spanish people have all of these. The black folks are still in the old times in Jennings, FL.

 Folkston, GA is a small town and almost like Jennings, FL. Please handle this very carefully.

 Thank you,

153

Ralph L. Watts

Mr. Watts:

Given the concerns you have expressed below, I am not willing to send out an email to our members. If I did, I could not guarantee the secrecy of the information or that it would NOT be disseminated to others. The Gate City Bar Association cannot guarantee that the information you have provided will be kept confidential, if we send it out. Considering you are afraid for your life, we simply will not take that risk.

I suggest that you contact the Georgia Legal Services Program in your area for assistance. The 2 offices closest to the counties you listed is below.

GLSP Brunswick and Waycross Regional Offices Contact Information

Brunswick Regional Office	Waycross Regional Office
1607 Union Street	506 Isabella Street
Brunswick, Georgia 31520	Waycross, Georgia 31501
(912) 264-7301 or	(912) 285-6181 or
1-877-808-0553	1-800-498-9508

Dear Atty. Phillips,

I would like to prepare a folder with all the information and send it to you.
First I will give you a quick rundown and your answer might be no.

A man named Joe Jordan purchase 17 acres of land many years ago. After a few years he gave his wife (Elizabeth) an acre of land. Elizabeth died after a few years. Joe (her husband) moved into her house.

After many more years Joe got sick. He had five or seven children. Two lived in Folkston on his land. No one would care for him, therefore one daughter (Lillie Mae) who lived near Bradenton, FL packed up her children and husband Willie and came to Folkston, GA. Year after year Lillie Mae took care of her Father.

Later Joe died. Lillie Mae did not know at first but Joe Jordan had willed all his land to Lillie Mae. The rest of the family was angry. Lillie Mae told them she would divide all the land among them if they help bury their father. No one hope so she had to mortgage the land to bury her father.

When she mortgage she divided the land suitable for the mortgage company.
Later I married her daughter (Rose) everything was going good. About two years after our marriage a divorce took place. Rose sold

me her share of the deed. When this happen the family got upset.
They wanted the land back.
They got an Attorney and said Lillie Mae forged Elizabeth deed and the
deed I have is no good. Remember Lillie Mae had mortgage part of the
acre to bury her father.

I was sold another part (87' of 200') of the 200'x200'.
I only have 87 feet of the 200 feet in length. I was told by other law
firms if they were correct they should have gone after Lillie Mae.
They also showed me the presentation they presented to the Court is
incorrect. Then I realized that is why at the first court meeting the
Judge would not accept it and said it must go to a Jury.

The second court meeting my Attorney was late and the two
Attorneys got together in a back room and coerce me into accepting
this ugly deal.
After I paid everybody these people will not give me a deed. They
know what went on is wrong and decide to wait until I die and
everything will go their way.

There are many ugly things that went on. They will surprise you.
I hope you will accept this case. Just to tell you what I was told. Two of
the Law Firms said this County does not have this kind of money but
they need a wakeup call. If I acquire an Attorney please ask him to
start suing for $150 millions. The County should have not let two
Attorneys from different counties come and conduct business
unlawfully. This case is unlawful.

Please do not send mail to my Folkston address. Yes I am afraid.

Thank you,

Ralph L. Watts
5813 Rover Drive
Jacksonville, FL 32244

I was about to lose or I had lost my mind. I just could not think

straight any longer.
----- Original Message -----
From: "Kim T. Phipps" <ktphipps@bomarphipps.com>
To: "'ralphwatts'" <ralphwatts@comcast.net>
Sent: Friday, July 02, 2010 5:06 PM
Subject: RE: Potential Client Inquiry from FindLaw FirmSite:
www.bomarphippslaw.com

Mr. Watts,

We would have to know more about the situation before we can
determine if we can help you. Please feel free to contact me at one of
the numbers below.

Kim T. Phipps, Esq.
BOMAR & PHIPPS, LLC
5447 Roswell Road, N.E.
Suite 100
Atlanta, Georgia 30342
(404) 593-2643 (Direct Dial)
(404) 841-6561 (Main Office)
(404) 841-9178 (Facsimile)
ktphipps@bomarphipps.com

157

-----Original Message-----
From: ralphwatts [mailto:ralphwatts@comcast.net]
Sent: Wednesday, June 30, 2010 5:27 PM
To: Kim T. Phipps
Cc: ralphwatts@comcast.net
Subject: Re: Potential Client Inquiry from FindLaw FirmSite:
www.bomarphippslaw.com

Small town (mean & ugly) Georgia

----- Original Message -----
From: "Kim T. Phipps" <ktphipps@bomarphipps.com>
To: <ralphwatts@comcast.net>
Sent: Wednesday, June 30, 2010 3:52 PM
Subject: RE: Potential Client Inquiry from FindLaw FirmSite:
www.bomarphippslaw.com
Mr. Watts,
Is the probate case in Georgia or Florida?

158

Kim T. Phipps, Esq.
BOMAR & PHIPPS, LLC
5447 Roswell Road, N.E.
Suite 100
Atlanta, Georgia 30342
(404) 593-2643 (Direct Dial)
(404) 841-6561 (Main Office)
(404) 841-9178 (Facsimile)
ktphipps@bomarphipps.com

CONFIDENTIALITY AND REPRESENTATION NOTICE: The pages comprising this e-mail
transmission contain privileged and confidential information. The information herein is solely for the use of the individual or entity recipient. Contact via email does not create an attorney-client relationship. Our law firm will not be representing you until the terms of
our representation are discussed, mutually agreed upon and memorialized in writing.

-----Original Message-----
From: ralphwatts@comcast.net [mailto:ralphwatts@comcast.net]
Sent: Wednesday, June 30, 2010 2:59 PM
To: ktphipps@bomarphipps.com
Subject: Potential Client Inquiry from FindLaw FirmSite:
www.bomarphippslaw.com

This inquiry originated from your FindLaw FirmSite:
www.bomarphippslaw.com

Comments: Hello,

I am from a small county in Georgia. I am writing this looking for an Attorney who is not afraid of other Attorneys.

I am involved in a Probate case and it like back in the 1920s or 1940s. I am 73 years old and they think I will not seek help.

Please I had three law firms look over this case and each tell me it is not the way to present a case to the court. I am looking for help but I do not want anyone here to find out. I am in Jacksonville, FL living with my daughter until I can get help. Please email me if you can help.

Thanks,

Ralph L. Watts

Preferred Contact Method: Email
Name: Ralph L.Watts
City: Jacksonville
State: Florida
Zip: 32244
Phone: 904-305-7224:
Email: ralphwatts@comcast.net
This email was initiated at the FindLaw FirmSite
www.bomarphippslaw.com. The
content of this email is provided by and is the responsibility of the person posting the email communication. Your email will not create an attorney-client relationship and will not necessarily be treated as privileged or confidential. You acknowledge that any reliance on material in email communications is at your own risk.

Mr. Watts,

You are certainly welcome to send the information over for my review. I will say, however, that in these situations it is usually better, if you can, to involve someone local who is familiar to the judge in whose court the matter is pending.

Kim T. Phipps, Esq.

BOMAR & PHIPPS, LLC

5447 Roswell Road, N.E.

I could not get any help from anybody. There I will now try an African-American attorney. I am sure he will understand my position.

I go online and see this advertisement of this big time African

American attorney in Atlanta, Georgia.

Maybe I can get some help from an African American attorney:

I send information to this guy.

ericsmith195@comcast.net;

Churchill Law Firm

161

Mr. Watts

Please call the office at 404-942-3667, so that we can discuss this matter further.

Eric Smith

Probate Case c/o Eric Smith

Dear Mr. Smith,

I received your message. My phone is not the best condition and I do apologize.

I am asking if we can communicate through emails and letters.

I would love to send you this case for evaluation. This case is in Georgia.

I thank you once again for your interest.

Sincerely,

Ralph L. Watts

5813 Rover Drive

Jacksonville, FL 32244

ralphwatts@comcast.net

From: ralphwatts [mailto:ralphwatts@comcast.net]
Sent: Sunday, July 18, 2010 5:19 PM
To: ktphipps@bomarphipps.com
Cc: ralphwatts@comcast.net

Subject: Probate

Mrs. Phillips,

I am very sorry but I did not get your last transmission on this case in Folkston, GA.

Did you want me to send you this case to look it over and see if you can help? Or maybe you decided not to review it.

Either way please let me know. I want to hurry and resolve this before the Court say I waited too long.

Thank you,

Ralph L. Watts

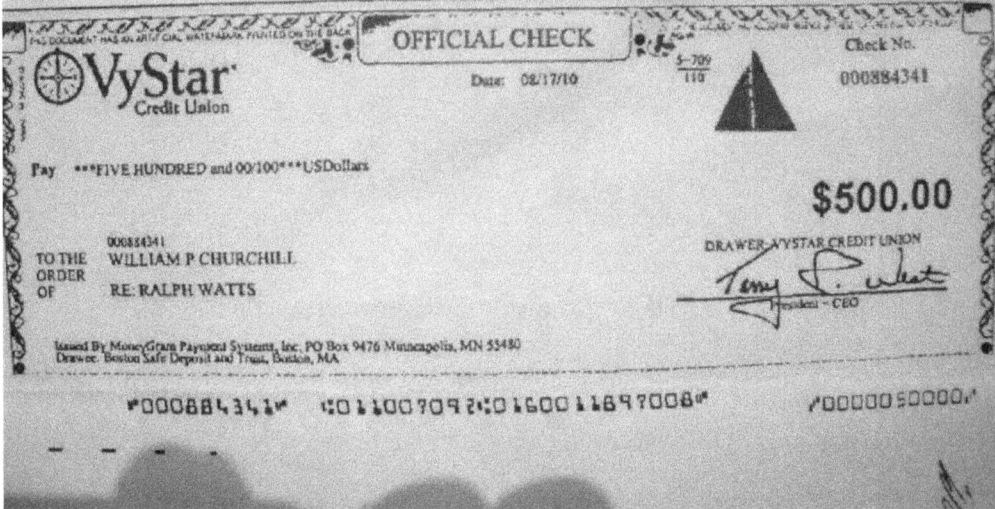

OFFICIAL CHECK

VyStar Credit Union

Date: 02/17/10

5-709
110

Check No.

000884341

Pay ***FIVE HUNDRED and 00/100*** USDollars

$500.00

00884341

TO THE ORDER OF

WILLIAM P CHURCHILL

RE: RALPH WATTS

DRAWER: VYSTAR CREDIT UNION

President - CEO

Issued By MoneyGram Payment Systems, Inc. PO Box 9476 Minneapolis, MN 55480
Drawer: Boston Safe Deposit and Trust, Boston, MA

I call Eric Smithy and ask about writing a letter to Robert's attorney.

He said that would be $500.00 to write Robert's attorney.

On August 17, 2010 I sent Cashier check to William Churchill.

I expected him to write the letter immediately.

Ralph L. Watts

P. O. Box 9464

Jacksonville, FL 32208

The Churchill Law Firm

Atlanta, GA.

Dear Mr. Churchill,

Thank you! I've been so upset lately I do not think I can last much longer.

The letter that I would like for you to write is to Robert Jordan attorney. I enclosed a letter that I wrote to him requesting the deed and an overpayment returned that was made to his client. (Robert Jordan) The Probate Judge got a copy also. I have not heard anything from them. I think they believe I do not know what to do or whether anyone will help me.

I am also sending you copies of the letters that I wrote to the Court. I tried my best to get this case heard. On our first court date the two Attorneys discuss this case to the Judge. I notice the Judge looked at the second page a long time. He told the Attorneys he cannot rule on this and for them to take it to a Jury. (They agreed).

The second court date my Attorney was late. When he did come; he and the other Attorney went into a back room for discussion. Within a few minutes the other attorney came out and told me my Attorney wanted to see me. I went in the back room and the first thing he said to me. "We have got to solve this case" He went on: "The best thing is for you to pay Robert $5,000.00 and this case is solved". I could not believe this, I had some witnesses for him to question and he just said "This is the best thing for you-I am going back to my office and type the papers for you to sign". "You can keep your house"

I left out the room with nothing but hurt. My Attorney is 85 years old and I should have known better to get him.

The next day I went to the Probate Judge office to speak with him. He seen the agony and frustration that I was experiencing. I could not hold things together, tears from my eyes I could not stop. I ran out his office.

A few days later I wrote the Probate Judge a letter an apologized for my actions. I received a letter from him on his closing he said <u>I can get relief in Superior Court</u>.

That is really what I wanted, this case to go to trial. I had three Law firms to look at this case. Each tells me this is the wrong presentation. Then I realize when the Superior Court Judge told the Attorneys he could not ruled on this case. He saw that the presentation was inadequate. That is the reason for them having me in the back office coercing me to accept their offer.

166

I would appreciate it if you look at this case. The last Attorney I spoke with here in Jacksonville said this is a lawsuit. What he told me makes sense. When Lillie may Harvey daddy died, she had to bury her daddy without any help from the brother (Robert Jordan) or sisters. She changed the structure of the land (including Elizabeth Jordan) without any one objecting so it could be mortgaged. If there was a problem, the family should have gone after Lillie May Harvey.

Two decades later when the property been rearrange and part mortgage they want to rename Elizabeth Jordan parcel. They cannot do this I was told it is against the law.

Mr. Churchill I do not want to bury you with my problems. But I believe there is plenty of money for you if you take this case. I believe they would try to settle out of Court because this would be embarrassing for them.

I want to tell you this; I purchase 100 shares from The Florida National Bank years ago.

This is what I put up for cash when I went to court. Before I gave them to my Attorney to help pay for this case I called the Bank and they said my shares was worth over $9400.00. My Attorney worried me to cash them. He needed some money. OK I signed for him to cash them and he said they had a value of $7400.00. This is $2000.00 less than a week ago. I do not have the money now but if you will please secretly check and find out what they were sold for. If they skim money off the top I will be really upset and will ask for a lawsuit. The 100 share Certificate was made out to me. Ralph Watts, from The First National Corp; Certificate #0563.

Mr. Churchill please help me with this. I am not in a hurry, just take your time. I just want things right. I was borne in a small town and grew up around this same stuff that is happening here. All we could say is "yes sir and no sir". If I were a young they probably would not do this, but they know I am old and was borne when they dominated us with fear. Please use my address above. In Folkston our mail be opened and I do not know who and no one can say anything.

One more thing I would like to ask you. If you decide to write the letter asking for the deed; please tell him to send it to you. If he sends it to me I know it will not be right.

I am saying these guys cannot be trusted.

Thank you very much,

Ralph L. Watts

I did not get an answer; this guy just forgot about me.

I sent this guy $500.00 to write a letter and the letter never was written.

Later, when I realized this attorney was a scammer I asked for my money back. He then says he is charging me for looking at some letters I sent him.

I sent him $500.00 to write a letter and that is what he was supposed to do.

He did not write the letter and I had to threaten him for him to recognize the money he received from me. Then and only then he asks what do I want him to do?

Can you believe this? He is an attorney with supposedly good knowledge.

He told me he charges me $500.00 to write that letter. I send the money and months later he asks what do I want him to do?

Track & Confirm FAQs

Label/Receipt Number: 0309 2880 0002 2877 6183

Class: First-Class Mail®

Service(s): Delivery Confirmation™

Status: Delivered

Your item was delivered at 8:57 am on August 20, 2010 in ATLANTA, GA 30309.

Enter Label/Receipt Number.

Enter Label / Receipt Number. 0309 2880 0002 2877 6183

Detailed Results:

Delivered, August 20, 2010, 8:57 am, ATLANTA, GA 30309

Arrival at Post Office, August 20, 2010, 6:22 am, ATLANTA, GA 30309

Processed through Sort Facility, August 19, 2010, 4:54 pm, ATLANTA, GA 30369

Processed through Sort Facility, August 18, 2010, 8:20 pm, JACKSONVILLE, FL 32218

Acceptance, August 18, 2010, 8:57 am, JACKSONVILLE, FL 32244

Track & Confirm by email

Get current event information or updates for your item sent to you or others by email.

Thursday, September 30, 2010

Ralph L. Watts

5813 Rover Drive

Jacksonville, FL 32244

William P. Churchill, III P.C.

The Promenade II

1230 Peachtree St. NE; Suite 1900

Atlanta, GA 30309

Dear Mr. Churchill,

This is the second notice I am writing for confirmation on the package that was sent to this address on August 20, 2010.. I need confirmation because there is a check involved.

Below is the USPO confirmation the package was delivered.

 Label/Receipt Number: 0309 2880 0002 2877 6183

Expected Delivery Date: August 20, 2010

Class: First-Class Mail®

Service(s): Delivery Confirmation™

Status: Delivered

171

Your item was delivered at 8:57 am on August 20, 2010 in ATLANTA, GA 30309.

Detailed Results:

Delivered, August 20, 2010, 8:57 am, ATLANTA, GA 30309

Arrival at Post Office, August 20, 2010, 6:22 am, ATLANTA, GA 30309

Processed through Sort Facility, August 19, 2010, 4:54 pm, ATLANTA, GA 30369

Processed through Sort Facility, August 18, 2010, 8:20 pm, JACKSONVILLE, FL 32218

Acceptance, August 18, 2010, 8:57 am, JACKSONVILLE, FL 32244

Please confirm that the package was received.

Thank you,

Ralph L. Watts

Confirmation of package receiveded

Sunday, November 14, 2010

Ralph L. Watts

5813 Rover Drive

Jacksonville, FL 32244

William P. Churchill

The Churchill Firm

The Promenade II

1230 Peachtree St; NE, Suite 1900

Atlanta, GA 30309

Dear Mr. Churchill,

A package was delivered to you at this address August 20, 2010.
The Post Office confirmed the package was delivered.

173

I would like written confirmation from you the package was received. Please confirm delivery of this package. A check

was enclosed.

If I do not hear from you by Wed, November 17, 2010; I will take the next step to resolve this matter.

Please reply to this email. I do not want to discuss this matter by phone. Just reply to this email. This is very important.

Thank you,

Ralph L. Watts

Can you imagine that? I sent this guy a check for $500.00 to write a letter

August 17, 2010.

Here it is almost December and the letter is not written. Actions of this nature cause people to really lose it and do something terrible. They do not know this person have been mistreated to the highest level.

As you see this man got all my money and done absolutely nothing.

Since he has done nothing maybe he can tell me something about my case. This is not for hire. The hire was for the letter writing.

November 26, 2010

Ralph L. Watts

P. O. Box 9464

Jacksonville, FL 32208

William P. Churchill, III, P.C.

The Promenade II

1230 Peachtree St. NE

Suite 1900

Atlanta, GA 30309-3578

Dear Mr. Churchill,

I appreciate the conversation we had on Wednesday. I think I send you so much stuff, its does not say what I want or really need.

If you look at the diagram I will try to explain it.

The 200 sq block is the property that all this is about. This is the property that Robert Jordan daddy deeded to his wife (Robert's mother).

Robert's daddy deeded his mother this 200'sq feet acre of land.

Robert's mother died. Robert's daddy moved into her house (his wife & Robert's mother).

He died but he had deeded all the land to his daughter Lillie Mae Harvey. Lillie Mae Harvey is Robert's sister.

As the years past Lillie May Harvey reshapes the land. She sold some and mortgaged some.

If you look at the diagram the 200 sq ft land is the land Robert was assigned as Executive by the Court.

The dotted line is the way Lillie Mae sold it to me. I have about 80 or 90 feet so off in the middle of the 200 ft sq footage.

They said Lillie Mae did not have the right to sell me this land and I do not own anything.

OK so I paid for this land and by the court made Robert the Executive he should have the right to execute a Warranty deed to me. I do not want to be in Court again about this property. A quick claim deed will leave me in the way for all kind of lawsuits.

Right now I do not have anything. I am waiting for Robert to issue me a deed to his mother's property. This is the fastest way to solve this problem. Issue me a warranty deed and pay back the money that was overpaid to him.

If not that then the next step is Court. I want him to pay your fees, the Attorney before you fees and the money I paid him. I think he will take the first option. All I want is a clear deed from Robert, which I am entitling too.

The other part of the land (rear of the 200 sq) Lillie Mae Harvey had full say and owner.

Robert does not have the say over the other part of land which Lillie Mae Harvey clearly owns.

So please if you can get Robert's Attorney to issue me a deed and pay back the over payment that was paid to him; my problem is solved.

Robert's mother passed away in Milledgeville, Georgia. I do not know if there was any more information on her illness.

This is the reason why I must settle this quickly and move. I say this to you quietly.

Again thank you for your help.

Ralph L. Watts

Ps. Again if there is a problem receiving a warranty deed I will settle for a quick claim if it fast and for the right property. (his mother's deed)

Subject: A Happier New Year

Tuesday, December 28, 2010

Ralph L. Watts

5813 Rover Drive

Jacksonville, FL 32244

William P. Churchill, III Atty

1230 Peachtree St. NE Ste 1900

Atlanta, GA 30309

Dear Mr. Churchill,

I was hoping I would have a Christmas gift of the deed to this property. Right now I am staying on land without a deed.

I know this is a bad time but I have to ask you this question.

Would it be a good thing if I go to the State Attorney office in Folkston and file Grand Larceny charges against Robert Jordan?

This guy sold me an acre of land for $5,000.00 and promise to give me a deed and he refused. I think when this happen the State call this Grand Larceny.

If this happen Robert could be forced to honor or give me the deed to his mother's (Elizabeth Jordan) property plus the money he owe for over payment.

If this is true the State might also pick up and continue the charges against him. Never-the-less I just want Elizabeth Jordan deed and the over payment made to him.

Please email me back with some idea.

Happy New Year,

Ralph L. Watts

Tuesday, January 18, 2011

Notified by Registered Mail.

Ralph L. Watts

P. O. Box 36

Folkston, GA 31537

William P. Churchill, III, PC

The Promenade II

1230 Peachtree St. NE

Suite 1900

Atlanta, GA 30309-3578

Dear Mr. Churchill,

I have decided not to wait any longer. It doesn't make sense for me to have $14,000 invested in one acre (value $2,000) and can not get a deed. I am tired of waiting and people just taking advantage of me.

As of today, Tuesday, January 18, 2011 do not do anything. I planned another way to get things done immediately. Therefore I am asking you to return the $500.00 you charge for writing a letter. The letter never was written and I am entitled for the return of this fee.

Please do not write a letter now. I have already put another plan into action. I hope you understand the frustrations I have gone through.

Never-the-less this matter is for the State Attorney Office. I am taking everything to him. I want a real Court to handle this.

Again have a great year,

Sincerely,

Ralph Watts

Wednesday, January 19, 2011 (Atty Beacon notified by Registered Mail.)

Ralph L. Watts

P. O. Box 36

Folkston, GA 31537

The State Attorney Office

Richard Currie, Atty

306 Albany Avenue

Waycross, GA 31501

Gary A. Beacon, Atty

Post Office Box 5880

St. Marys, GA 31558

Dear Mr. Beacon,

I sent you a letter on May 10, 2010. I explain to you that your client (Robert Jordan) was overpaid $103.03. I also ask you to make sure the deed to Elizabeth Jordan property (1 acre) was sent to me. I paid your Client $5,000.00 plus 8% interest. Now your client owes 8% on $103.03 from June 15, 2010. February 15, 2011 he owes me $115.33.

I waited over seven (7) months and nothing happen. Now I am sending you another letter.

This letter I am explaining that thirty (30) days from the date of this letter if I do not have all that belong to me I will go to the State Attorney Office and file grand larceny charges against your client.

I have had enough of this case. In the beginning I paid $5,000.00 for this acre to Lillie Harvey. Then her brother came and got $5,000.00 from me. Then the Attorney I had which did nothing got about $3,700.00 out of me. All this money I paid out for an acre of land worth only $2,000.00 in the beginning. (Scamming)

The State law states an Attorney may not charge a client no more that 10-15% of the value of the estate. This estate was $2,000.00. (One acre of land) This did not include me in this law. I was charged what they wanted without attending to the law.

I am mostly hurt because I took you to be a Christian man. I had no idea that you would let this happen to anyone. Now one thing I want you to believe: Thirty days from the date of this letter I will be in the State Attorney's Office filing grand Larceny charges against your client.

I am also sending a copy of this letter to him so he can expect me.

Happy New Year,

Ralph L. Watts

Thursday, February 17, 2011

Ralph L. Watts

Post Office Box 36

Folkston, GA 31537

Honorable Robert F. Phillips, Judge

Charlton Probate Court

100 South Third Street

Folkston, GA 31537

Dear Honorable Judge Phillips,

I do understand you made Robert Jordan Administrator of Elizabeth Jordan Property.

As Administrator he has the obligation to issue a deed when this property was paid.

It has been several months waiting after a notification was sent to his Attorney.

He refused to issue Elizabeth Jordan deed to me. Therefore, I am seeking help from the State Attorney's Office.

I paid Lillie Mae Harvey $5,000.00; now her brother came along and got another $5,000.00. The Attorney I had got about $3,700.00 which he did nothing. This is about $14,000.00 I paid for one acre of land. (In the beginning it was worth $2,000.00). Now I do not have a deed because Robert Jordan refuses to issue it. This is too much money to play around with.

This is not something against your office. I just like for everyone to know what is going on. A copy of the letter to Robert Jordan's Attorney is enclosed.

Thank you and Happy New Year,

Ralph L. Watts

cc. State Attorney

"   File

Thursday, February 17, 2011

Ralph L. Watts

P. O. Box 36

Folkston, GA 31537

The State Attorney Office

Richard Currie, Atty

306 Albany Avenue

Waycross, GA 31501

William P. Churchill, III, PC

The Promenade II

1230 Peachtree St. NE; Suite 1900

Atlanta, GA 30309-3578

Dear Mr. Churchill,

You charged me $500.00 to write Robert Jordan attorney a letter requesting answers about my deed. This letter never was written. In fact it took a threaten letter for you to acknowledge the money was received.

I sent you an email December 28, 2010, January 10, 2011 and a Registered Letter January 18, 2011. You still refuse to answer any of these letters. I call several times before these letters and left messages requesting about the letter that was never written.

You are an Officer of the Court. I do expect you to do the right thing. I sent you $500.00 on August 20, 2010 just to write one letter. It was never written. Therefore on January 18, 2011 I sent you a letter (Registered mail) stopping all actions and to return the fee. I spoke with you less than two (2) minutes long ago once on the phone. If you charge me $50.00 for these two minutes that is OK. That leaves a balance of $450.00 returnable fee.

I do not want to converse on the phone. Sometimes we forget what we say and later deny everything. Mail is something that hands on. Please send me the balance of the fee. I do not have $450.00 to give away for nothing. Please for God's sakes do not say you did all other things to keep my fee. That is wrong and when wrong things happen, it has a way of coming back. Send me my balance fee. PLEASE!!!!

Thank you,

Ralph L. Watts

Cc: State Attorney

"   File

Saturday, February 19, 2011

Ralph L. Watts

P. O. Box 36

Folkston, GA 31537

The State Attorney Office

Richard Currie, Atty

306 Albany Avenue

Waycross, GA 31588

Dear Sir or Madam;

Your office have received letters from me because I have no other way to bring this Cause of Action Forward.

I am involved in a lawsuit in Charlton County. (Civil Action 05V=228) I had other Attorneys to look at the paperwork that were presented. They were astonish to know the Court accepted these papers in the form it was presented. I told them the Judge did not rule and for it to be taken before a Jury; maybe he knew the presentation was incorrect.

I was also told if a crime have been committed to take it to the State's Attorney office. Therefore I am asking for your help. Please let me file a complaint with your office. After you examine the paperwork and find criminal elements, your course of actions would be pleasing to me.

I really do not understand why and how someone can think a person can buy an acre and you do not give them a deed to the property. I am seventy-four (74) years old and the Attorneys have taken all my life saving. I am asking you to please help if you can.

189

Please send a letter on what I should do.

Thank you,

Ralph L. Watts

I received this letter from Robert Jordan attorney dated March 2, 2011

190

Bacon Law Firm, P.C.

Post Office Box 5880
St. Marys, Georgia 31558

Gary A. Bacon, Attorney

87 Hawthorn Lane, Suite B

Telephone 912 882-7322
Facsimile 912 882-8017

Email: gbacon@baconlawfirm.com
Website: baconlawfirm.com

March 2, 2011

Mr. Ralph Watts
Post Office Box 36
Folkston, Georgia 31537

Dear Mr. Watts:

This is to respond to a series of letters which you have sent to my office, the most recent one on Wednesday, January 19, 2011 by registered mail.

Please understand that I am not your attorney and have never been your attorney, therefore I am not under any duty to provide documents or information to you concerning any legal matter which you are involved in.

As you and I both know, you had a law firm representing you during this legal action and you should be directing your questions to them concerning any issues with their performance.

However, I am sending you a copy of a Quitclaim Deed which Mr. Robert Jordan signed on the 16th day of October 2008, which was mailed to your attorney's firm for filing. We were not responsible for the filing of this deed. If the deed has not been filed, I suggest you contact your law firm to see what the status of the deed is, or contact the courthouse to see if the deed has been filed.

Also enclosed is a Petition for Approval of Settlement. This petition was submitted by myself to request settlement of this matter, since Mr. Robert Jordan was administrator of the Elizabeth Jordan estate.

Also enclosed is an Order of Approval of Settlement, which was signed by your attorney, Mr. James B. McGee, and signed by me individually, and was approved by Judge Robert Phillips on the 21st day of July, 2008.

There was a deed to secure debt in this matter, which if you have paid all that you should have paid and would submit a request in writing to Mr. Jordan to sign a cancellation of this matter, I am sure he would be glad to do that for you.

He is not under any duty to provide you with any deed or any additional information other than the cancellation of that deed to secure debt, if in fact you have paid it off.

As concerning any balances you may or may not have overpaid, that is a matter you would have to take up directly with Mr. Jordan since I no longer represent him in this matter.

I hope this will satisfy your mind as to the concerns you have in this matter.

With kind personal regards, I remain,

Sincerely,

Bacon Law Firm, P.C.

Gary A. Bacon, Esq.

Enclosures
GAB/jec

CC: Mr. Robert Jordan

What I want to show you next is the deed that Robert Jordan attorney cooked up.

The law is no one can change the name on a deed but the maker. He sent me a deed just what Lillie Mae Harvey gave me. He is an attorney and he should know better than to do that. This deed is phony and the maker of this phony deed should be prosecuted.

If I gave a phony deed to anyone I will go to jail. The deed that I have is phony. I would like to know someone to prove that it isn't.

They said themselves that Lillie Mae Harvey cannot change the Title on a deed. Therefore it reverses itself to the original title.

193

Plaintiff prays that this court will approve this Settlement of Civil Action File # 05V-0228, pending in Superior Court of Charlton County, Georgia.

Respectfully submitted this 14th day of July, 2008.

                                        Gary A. Bacon
                                        Attorney for Administrator
                                        Robert Jordan
                                        State Bar Number: 030713

Post Office Box 5880
St. Marys, Georgia 31558
912 882-7322

payment of $500.00 due April 15, 2008, and monthly payments of the balance of $200.00 per month for 24 months and one final payment of $91.97 at a rate of 8% per month, secured by a second mortgage on the property which is the subject of this dispute. A legal description of said property is attached as Exhibit A.

The executor will simultaneously execute a Quit Claim Deed from the Estate to Mr. Ralph Watts. Mr. Ralph Watts will simultaneously execute a Deed to Secure Debt and Promissory Note to the Estate of Elizabeth Jordan for $4500.00 after receiving the $500.00 down payment.

Said funds will be applied to reimburse the Administrator for money which he paid for attorney fees in taking this action in Probate Court and Superior Court.

194

$4500.00 (Loan Amount)   Folkston, Georgia   Date of Loan : April 15, 2008

FOR VALUE RECEIVED, Ralph Watts (borrower) promises to pay to the order of Robert Jordan, Administrator of the Elisabeth Jordan Estate, (lender) the principal sum of FOUR THOUSAND FIVE HUNDRED ($4,500.00) Dollars, in legal tender of the United States, with interest thereon from date at the rate of EIGHT (8%) per centum per annum, on the unpaid balance until paid, in ONE installment, due as follows:

In twenty-four (24) payments of two hundred dollars ($200.00) per month and one final payment of ninety-one and 97/100 dollars ($91.97).

Principal and interest are payable to Robert Jordan, Administrator of the Elisabeth Jordan Estate (lender) at the following address: Route 2 Box 4098, Folkston, Georgia 31537, or at such other place as the holder hereof may designate in writing.

Should any installment not be paid when due, or should the maker, or makers, hereof fail to comply with any of the terms or requirements of a security deed of even date herewith, conveying title to real property located in N/A and N/A attached as security for this indebtedness, the entire unpaid principal sum evidenced by this note, with all accrued interest, shall, at the option of the holder, and without notice to the undersigned become due and may be collected forthwith, time being of the essence of this contract. It is further agreed that failure of the holder to exercise this right of accelerating the maturity of the debt, or indulgence granted from time to time, shall in no event be considered as a waiver of such right of acceleration or stop the holder from exercising such right.

In case this note is collected by law, as through an attorney at law, all costs of collection, including fifteen per centum (15%) of the principal and interest as attorney fees, shall be paid by the maker hereof.

And each of us, whether maker, endorse, guarantor, surety, hereby severally waives and renounces, for himself and family, any and all exemption rights either of us, or the family of either of us, may have under or by virtue of the Constitution or laws of Georgia, or any other State, or the United States, as against this debt or any renewal thereof; and each further waives demand, protest and notice of demand, protest and non-payment.

In case of default in the payment of any one of the aforesaid installments, and in case the holder of this note should elect, on account of such default, to declare the unpaid balance of the principal sum due and payable, said principal sum, or so much thereof as may remain unpaid at the time of such default, shall bear interest at the rate of eight per centum (8%) per annum from the date of such default.

This contract is to be construed in all respects and enforced according to the laws of the State of Georgia.

WITNESS my hand and seal this 21st day of July, 2008.

_____

Ralph Watts

195

Please return to:
Gary A. Bacon
Attorney at Law
Post Office Box 5880
St. Marys, Georgia 31558

STATE OF GEORGIA   DEED TO SECURE DEBT
COUNTY OF CAMDEN

THIS INDENTURE, Made the _____ of JULY, in the year of our Lord two thousand e
between Ralph Watts of the County of Charlton and State of Georgia, whose address is
_P._I._B#36___Fellarm_GA___31557___, as party of the first pa
hereinafter called Grantor, and Robert Jordan, Administrator of the Elisabeth Jordan Estate, S
of Georgia, as Party of the second part, hereinafter called Grantee, whose address is Route 2 I
4098, Folkston, Georgia 31537.

WITNESSETH, That Grantor, for the consideration hereinafter set forth, in hand paid
and before the sealing and delivery of these presents, and receipt whereof is hereby
acknowledged, has granted, bargained, sold, alienated, conveyed and confirmed, and by these
presents does grant, bargain, sell, alien, convey and confirm unto said Grantee, the following
described real property, to wit:

ALL that certain lot, tract or parcel of land situate, lying and being in the 32nd
G.M. District of Charlton County, Georgia, containing one (1) acre, more or less,
having the following metes and bounds:

BEGINNING at the point on the lane leading from the Gibson Post Road to the
Old Joe Jordan House, said point being on the westerly edge of said lane, and also
being the northeasterly corner of lands owned by Alberta Farlow, thence running
westwardly along the northerly land line of lands of Alberta Farlow a distance of
210 feet to a point (said point being the northwesterly corner of lands of said
Alberta Farlow); thence running northwardly in a straight line parallel to the
westerly right-of-way line of the aforesaid lane leading from the Gibson Post
Road to the Old Joe Jordan House a distance of 210 feet to a point; thence running
eastwardly in a straight line parallel to the aforesaid northerly land line of lands of
Alberta Farlow a distance of 210 feet to a point on the westerly right-of-way line
of the aforementioned lane; thence running southwardly along the said westerly
right-of-way line of said lane a distance of 210 feet back to the place or point of
beginning.

Said lot or parcel of land hereby conveyed is in the shape of a square, each side
being 210 feet in length, and is bounded as follows: Northwardly and
Westwardly by lands of Joe Jordan; Eastwardly by the aforementioned lane
leading from the Gibson Post Road to the Old Joe Jordan House (said lane being
the property of Joe Jordan); and Southwardly by lands of Alberta Farlow.

Said lot or parcel above described is a part and portion of that certain tract of land
conveyed to Joe Jordan by J. W. Buchanan's Executor in deed dated August 1,
1944, recorded in the public land records of Charlton County, Georgia, in Deed
Book "2", page 82; specific reference being hereby made to said deed and the
record thereof for description and all other legal purposes.

and also described as:

196

Another attorney told me this guy either don't know any better or just taking me for a ride.

The next part is Lillie Mae Harvey's deed these Bozos using/they know this is wrong. They are trying to give me a deed for property that is not Elizabeth Jordan. That is why this deed is phony. I explained this to The District Attorney but he refused to look into this case.

I wonder if I had done this (gave someone a phony deed) where would I be? In jail---I becha!!!!!

Why people want be loyal and decent?

197

All that tract or parcel of land situate, lying and being in the 32nd G. M. District of Charlton County, Georgia, and being more particularly described according to that certain plat prepared by Merlin J. Tomberlin and Associates, GA Registered Land Surveyor, dated August 21, 1993, and recorded in Plat Book D at page 230, Public Records of Charlton County, Georgia and being further designated on said plat as that certain tract containing 1.0 acres and being shown as lands now or formerly Elizabeth Jordan.

THIS CONVEYANCE is made under the provisions of the existing code of the State of Georgia with regard to the sale of property to secure debts, and to pass the title of the property described into the said Grantee, the debt hereby secured being evidence by one note dated July __31__, 200__8__, or any notes given in renewal thereof, in the principal amount of **four thousand five hundred and no/100 ($4,500.00), bearing interest at the rate of 8% per annum, due and payable in twenty-five installments, twenty-four installments of principal and interest of $200.00 per month and one final payment of $91.97 on April 15, 2010,** all in accord with the terms and conditions of said note.

This conveyance is given to secure, not only the within stated indebtedness, but as well as any and all other indebtedness now owing or which may hereafter be owing by Grantor herein to Grantee herein, however incurred, and all renewals of the whole or any part of the note or indebtedness hereby secured, including a note or notes changing the time and manner of payment of said indebtedness, and all extensions of said note and indebtedness, in whole or in part, so long as this deed remains of force and effect, and the word "indebtedness", as used herein, shall mean both direct and indirect debts and obligations, as principal, endorser, guarantor, or otherwise. It is the intention of the parties to create a perpetual or indefinite security interest in the real property described herein pursuant to the Official Code of Georgia Annotated section 44-14-80(a)(2) and to agree that title shall not revert to the Grantor herein for a period of 20 years from the date of maturity of this instrument. Any one of several persons named as grantee herein of their assigns may receive payment of the secured indebtedness and execute a valid cancellation of reconveyance hereof. No release of any part of the property herein described or extension of all or any part of the indebtedness hereby secured, shall affect the personal liability of any person upon the indebtedness hereby secured, nor the priority of this instrument.

TO HAVE AND TO HOLD the said bargained property with all and singular the rights, members and appurtenances thereto appertaining, to the only proper use, benefit and behoof of Grantee, in fee simple and Grantor hereby covenants that Grantor is lawfully seized and possessed of said property, and has a good right to convey it, and it is unencumbered; and Grantor hereby conveys the said bargained property to Grantee, against Grantor, and against all and every other person or persons shall and will WARRANT AND FOREVER DEFEND.

Should the indebtedness hereby secured be paid according to the tenor and effect thereof when same shall become due and payable, and should Grantor perform all covenants, herein contained, then this deed shall be canceled and surrendered, it being intended by the parties hereto that this instrument shall operate as a deed and not as a mortgage.

The Grantor covenants and agrees, so long as any indebtedness secured hereby shall remain unpaid to keep the property and all improvements thereon in as good condition as now exists, natural wear and tear excepted, and also not to the demolish, destroy, or remove any permanent structure now existing on the premises or make any alteration thereon that would constitute a structural change without the written consent of the Grantee; to pay all taxes and assessments that may be liens upon said property, as they become due; and to keep the improvements on said property fully insured against loss by fire and other hazards as may, from time to time, be required by Grantee in amounts and companies and with mortgage clause approved by Grantee, and shall deliver the policies of insurance and any renewals thereof to the said Grantee; and that any tax, assessment, prior tax lien or premium of insurance, not paid when due by Grantor may be paid by the Grantee, and any sum so paid shall be added to the amount of said principal debt as part thereof, shall draw interest from the time of said payment at the rate of eighteen percent per annum, and shall, with interest, be covered by the security of this deed.

AND Grantor hereby covenants and agrees that in case of any default in any partial payment of said indebtedness or in the due performance of any of the covenants herein expressed to be performed by Grantor, then and in that event, the entire amount of said principal

198

rights and powers herein granted to the grantee shall inure to and include his, her or its heirs, administrators, executors, successors and assigns, and all obligations herein imposed on the Grantor shall extend to and include Grantor's heirs, administrators, executors, successors and assigns.

IN WITNESS WHEREOF, the party of the first part has hereunto set hand and affixed seal, and delivered these presents, the day and year above written.

Ralph Watts

Signed, sealed, and delivered this 21st day of July 2008, in the presence of:

Witness

Notary Public

199

GRANTOR: RALPH WATTS
LENDER: Robert Jordan, Administrator of the Elisabeth Jordan Estate
DATE OF SECURITY DEED: July 21, 2008

WAIVER OF BORROWER'S RIGHTS

By execution of this paragraph, Grantors expressly: (1) Acknowledge the Right to Accelerate the debt and the Power of Attorney given herein to lender to sell the premises by nonjudicial foreclosure upon default by Grantors without any judicial hearing and without any notice other than such notice as is required to be given under the provisions thereof; (2) Waive any and all rights to which Grantors may have under the fifth and fourteenth amendments to the Constitution of the United States, the various provisions of the Constitution for the several states, or by reason of any other applicable law to notice and to judicial hearing prior to the exercise by lender of any right or remedy herein provided to lender, except such notice as is specifically required to be provided thereunder; (3) Acknowledge that Grantors have read this deed and specifically this paragraph and the foreclosure provisions of the deed and any and all questions regarding this legal effect of said deed and its provisions have been explained fully to Grantor and Grantor has been afforded an opportunity to consult with counsel of Grantor's choice prior to executing this deed; (4) Acknowledge that all waivers of the aforesaid rights of Grantor has been made knowingly, intentionally and willingly by Grantor as part of a bargained-for loan transaction; and (5) Agree that the provisions hereof are incorporated into and made a part of the security deed.

Read and agreed by Grantor:

_____
Ralph Watts, Grantor

Signed, sealed and delivered in the presence of:

_____
Witness

_____
Notary Public

Before me the undersigned attesting officer personally appeared the undersigned closing attorney, who having been first duly sworn to law, states under oath as follows:

In closing the above loan, but prior to the execution of the Deed to Secure Debt and "Waiver of Borrower's Rights" by the Borrower(s), I reviewed with and explained to the Borrower(s) the terms and provisions of the Deed to Secure Debt and particularly the provisions thereof authorizing the Lender to sell the secured property by a nonjudicial foreclosure under a power of sale, together with the "Waiver of Borrower's Rights" and informed the Borrower (s) of Borrower's rights under the Constitution of the State of Georgia and the Constitution of the United States to notice and a judicial hearing prior to such foreclosure in the absence of a knowing, intentional and willing contractual waiver by Borrower (s) rights. "Waiver or Borrower's Rights."

Based on said review with and explanation to the Borrower (s), it is my opinion that Borrower(s) knowingly, intentionally and willingly executed the Waiver of Borrower(s) constitutional rights to notice and judicial hearing prior to any such nonjudicial foreclosure.

_____
James B. McGee, Closing Attorney

Signed, sealed and delivered in the presence of:

_____
Witness

_____
Notary Public

200

THE PROBATE COURT OF CHARLTON COUNTY

STATE OF GEORGIA

In Re: Estate of Elizabeth Jordan
ROBERT J. JORDAN, Administrator

Order of Approval of Settlement

Robert Jordan, Administrator of the Elisabeth Jordan Estate, having petitioned this Court for an order approving the settlement of Civil Action File # 05V-0228, pending in Superior Court of Charlton County, Georgia. Said case is styled ROBERT JORDON, as Administrator of the Estate of ELIZABETH JORDAN, Plaintiff, vs. RALPH WATTS, Defendant. All parties having agreed to the settlement which was approved by their attorneys as evidenced by the signatures of the attorneys to this order, said settlement is hereby approved with the terms as follows:

In exchange for the payment of $5000.00 dollars, payable with an initial down payment of $500.00 due April 15, 2008, and monthly payments of the balance of $200.00 per month for 24 months and one final payment of $91.97 at a rate of 8% per month, secured by a second mortgage on the property which is the subject of this dispute. A legal description of said property is attached as Exhibit A.

The executor will simultaneously execute a Quit Claim Deed from the Estate to Mr. Ralph Watts. Mr. Ralph Watts will simultaneously execute a Deed to Secure Debt and Promissory Note to the Estate of Elizabeth Jordan for $4500.00 after receiving the

201

$500.00 down payment.

Said funds will be applied to reimburse the Administrator for money which he paid for attorney fees in taking this action in Probate Court and Superior Court.

So ordered this 21st of July, 2008.

_____
Honorable Robert F. Phillips
Probate Judge, Charlton County, Georgia

Order consented to by:

_____
Gary A. Bacon attorney for Administrator
Robert Jordan

_____
James B. McGee, attorney for Ralph Watts

202

OFFICE OF THE DISTRICT ATTORNEY
WAYCROSS JUDICIAL CIRCUIT

CURRIE
ney

306 Albany Avenue
Waycross, Georgia 31501

March 7, 2011

Mr. Ralph L. Watts
P.O. Box 36
Folkston, GA 31537

Dear Mr. Watts:

I am in receipt of your letter dated February 19, 2011. I do r
manpower or resources that allow me to investigate criminal activity. Ins
office prosecutes cases after they are investigated by a law enforcement

If a crime has been committed, I would advise you to report that
activity to the appropriate law enforcement agency — either the Folksto
Department (if it occurred in the jurisdiction of the city) or the Charlton
Sheriff's Office. If you do not get satisfaction there, you may also d
contact the Charlton County Magistrate Court.

Sincerely,

Richard E. Currie
District Attorney

March 4, 2011 I received this letter from Churchill.

I received warnings this guy would take your money.

Attorneys have a cheesy way of explaining their position.

Wednesday, March 09, 2011

Gary A Bacon, Atty

Post office Box 5880

St. Mary's, GA 31558

Dear Mr. Bacon,

I am in receipt of your letter dated March 02, 2011.

First I want to apologize for all the questions and answers I was expecting from you. I had no idea that you had discontinue Robert Jordan's service. It was my understanding when you have a client; it is your client until the case is settled.

I also want to apologize for letting my feelings of expectation range high as they did about you. When I read your book I thought what was said was truthful. Therefore I expected the best and righteousness from some-one with thoughts of this nature.

I took this deed you sent me to another Law Firm. They confirmed what I knew all along. Robert Jordan cannot give me a deed for land I already own.

Judge Phillips told me he made Robert Jordan Executor of Elizabeth Jordan property only. That means that property Lillie Harvey truly owns cannot be executed in this deed. Remember "Only the maker can change the Title"

Elizabeth Jordan has a 210 ft. sq lot. She did not have what you and Robert Jordan put together. That is the reason you all did not want this case to go to court. You and my attorney coerce me into signing this ugly agreement.

But don't you worry I will not bother you again. I am going to find an Attorney who is honest and I can trust he will do the right thing. I been thru hell with all the frustrations and ugliness this case had cause me. This case was setup wrong, process wrong and I am not going to keep quiet about it. I intend to let the world know about this case.

Again I apologize and am not angry with you. I will not let my love for God get overpowered by unrighteous doings.

Thank you,

Ralph L. Watts

cc: Judge Phillips

   State Attorney Office

Attorney Bacon got this letter. He knows I am right about him changing the Name on the deed. The law is only the Maker can change the deed.

He claims Lillie Mae Harvey cannot change the deed. If she cannot he certainly cannot. At least she has something to show she is entitled to all his land.

The kicker is Lillie Mae Harvey cannot change the deed but Robert Jordan and his attorney can. Come on a child knows better. Everybody is not that dumb.

It very hard for me to believe that someone that is Religious can make

Unrighteous deals. Bacon supposes to have written a book entitle Miracle in Michigan.

If you read this book you would say this man is a man that believes in the Holy Bible. That is the reason I told the Georgia Bar to speak with this guy.

Man I really stuck my foot in it. I thought this guy was alright.

He gave the little book to McGee. McGee said he does not read anything like that and gave it to me. I was grateful that I had met someone in Christ.

Maybe some people think its OK to treat others unjustly. I recognize others when they get in heir unjustly acts. You cannot be a winner when nothing else matters.

Well I am still looking for help.

Monday, March 28, 2011

Ralph L. Watts

5813 Rover Drive

Jacksonville, FL 32244

Kathleen Holbrook Cold

One Independent Drive

Suite 2301

Jacksonville, FL 32202

Dear Mrs. Cold,

I am involved in a property dispute in Folkston, Georgia. This is one of those deals where the attorneys do as they please without regard for the law. I am supposed to keep quite but an online Law Firm said I should take it to court.

I purchase an acre of land which costs $5,000.00 and I cannot get a deed issued for the acre.

Please if it's possible that I can come in and explain what happen.

I also learned from online this might not make it to a courtroom. It would be too embarrassing to let this get to a Jury.

I really need your help. My phone isn't working properly. Sometimes it rings but I can always received messages. 904-305-7224

I appreciate it very much if you can help me out of this mess.

Thank you,

Ralph L. Watts

I am now really craving for help.

 I thank you very much Ralph To dr.mac5@comcast.net

From: Ralph Watts (ralphwatts@hotmail.com)

Sent: Mon 4/11/11 2:01 PM

To: dr.mac5@comcast.net

Sir I thank you very much

Hide details dr.mac5@comcast.netdr.mac5@comcast.net

Send email

Find email Add to contacts Mr. Watts.......Please contact attorney Nathaniel Haugebrook at 1-229-560-1502, in Valdosta Georgia, hopefully he will be able to assist you. Dr. McIntosh To Ralph Watts, Thomas Raines, michael

From: dr.mac5@comcast.net

Sent: Mon 4/11/11 10:09 AM

To: Ralph Watts (ralphwatts@hotmail.com)

Cc: Thomas Raines (tcraines@comcast.net); michael (michael@urbanmarketingnetwork.com)

Mr. Watts.......Please contact attorney Nathaniel Haugebrook at 1-229-560-1502, in Valdosta Georgia, hopefully he will be able to assist you.

Dr. McIntosh

4/10/11 Show

Look like I might get some help

 Ralph Watts

Sir I thank you so much. I was born in a small town and know how things were back in the 50's. When this happen it brought back memories that really hurt.

Please I will appreciate it very much if you

To dr.mac5@comcast.net

From: Ralph Watts (ralphwatts@hotmail.com)

Sent: Sun 4/10/11 8:04 PM

To: dr.mac5@comcast.net

dr.mac5@comcast.net Add to contacts Mr. Watts I will look into this for you on Monday. Dr. McIntosh President Sent via Blackberry from T-Mobile To ralphwatts@hotmail.com

From: dr.mac5@comcast.net

Sent: Sun 4/10/11 4:37 PM

To: ralphwatts@hotmail.com

Mr. Watts I will look into this for you on Monday. Dr. McIntosh President Sent via Blackberry from T-Mobile

Friday, April 15, 2011

Ralph L. Watts

5813 Rover Drive

Jacksonville, FL 32244

Nathaniel Haugebrook, Atty.

104 East Adair Street

Valdosta, GA 31601

Dear Mr. Haugebrook,

First I want to apologize for my terrible telephone conversation. I retired from Greyhound as a driver. I drove at midnight and when the passengers go to sleep and I get sleepy, I would put one of those speaker phones in my ear and turn up the volume. This is supposed to keep me awake but it ruined my hearing. I catch myself speaking loud because I have a hearing problem.

I am sending you some copies to examine. I placed numbers on them trying to keep my information in order.

Copy 1 shows what the county has on record. I put a dotted line where Elizabeth Jordan property supposes to be. This is a 210 ft sq acre. This acre is what Judge Phillips made Robert Jordan Executive of.

Copy #2 is pretty much the same as copy #1. The dotted lines are the property of Elizabeth Jordan.

Copy #3 is the correction deed for deed filed 04-22-1997.

Copy #4 is a letter to the Tax Assessors to also make corrections.

Copy #5 is a letter to the court trying to get some relief from this course of action.

Copy #6 is a letter to the State Attorney's office seeking help.

Copy #7 is a letter to the Probate Judge.

Copy #8 is a letter from the Probate Judge.

Robert Jordan wants me to have property that owns by Lillie Mae Harvey. He does not have the authority to deed me property that is legally owned by someone else. All kinds of lies he told in the Court Documents. How he built his mother's house and Mr. Harvey said he was a drunk. I just needed an Attorney to pick these things apart.

Elizabeth Jordan died around 1972. She was at Milledgeville, GA. That is the reason for the Jordan's divorce. The seeds from Elizabeth Jordan are in a few of their children. That is the reason I have to move.

I will tell you what I learn online from difference attorneys. If that property was mortgage years before and there was no Probate executed; you cannot probate on the second sale.

A part of this acre was mortgaged to a company years before I came along. Now I have paid for someone else land. They said the Circuit Court Judge would not rule because of the improprieties in the presentation. He knew you cannot probate one case for another. The Probate Judge should have caught this and stopped the action.

That is the reason why the Attorneys coerce me into accepting their agreement. They stated this will keep Robert Jordan from taking my land. This was a setup to get money from me.

I am also sending a letter from the Probate Judge stating my relief will be in the Superior Court (#8). I will also send you a copy of the presentation Wednesday when I get it copied.

I have many letters, notes, etc. if you need them. Please help me if you can. Any settlement will do. (Lawsuit will be better).

212

163 WEST MAIN STREET • POST OFFICE BOX 927 • DOTHAN, ALABAMA 36302
TELEPHONE: (334) 793-1555 • FAX: (334) 793-8280
WWW.COCHRANFIRM.COM

April 20, 2012

Ralph Watts
P.O. Box 9464
Jacksonville, FL 32208

RE: Potential Claim

Dear Mr. Watts:

This serves to express our appreciation for your permitting our firm to revi~
potential claim. After reviewing the information provided, our firm has reached the ~
to respectfully decline representation. Our decision should not be inferred to indica~
of merit in the case. You have every right to secure a second legal opinion ~
encourage you to do so.

Please be aware that state and federal laws place a strict time limit on the ~
pursue an action. If an action is not filed, or the matter settled, within the ap~
statue period, you will lose the right to pursue a claim. If you do not know of ~
attorney, you may telephone the Florida State Bar LRS at 1-904-399-5780. T~
provide information on how to contact an attorney in your area who might be able ~
you.

Although we are not undertaking to represent you in this matter, we appre~
opportunity to review your case, and we wish you the best possible outcome. Pl~
free to contact us again should the need arise. For the firm, I am

Sincerely,

THE COCHRAN FIRM-DOTHA~

Date: Mon, 9 May 2011 15:48:21 +0000

From: dr.mac5@comcast.net

To: ralphwatts@hotmail.com

Subject: Re: My last request

Mr. Watts you need to get an attorney in the county where this matter took place. An attorney here is not going to help you. You matter is a superior court matter, not probate. I will try and find attorney's who are real estate people to help.

Dr. Mac

----- Original Message -----

From: "Ralph Watts" <ralphwatts@hotmail.com>

To: "dr mac5" <dr.mac5@comcast.net>

Sent: Sunday, May 8, 2011 7:18:46 PM

Subject: RE: My last request

Yes Sir; I live here in Jacksonville mostly because I am afraid to live by this family of people. I go there in the day for an hour or so but I come back here before dark. (Their grandmother passed away in the crazy house)

I had no idea what I was getting into years ago.

I drove for greyhound; I met this good looking lady. I just went berserk and out of control. This was Lillie Mae Harvey's daughter. We dated a short while and I am ready for marriage. Her father was a big time Deacon and mother was a Mother in the church plus she was a church member. I was sure this was a Christian family.

I never have been so wrong. They needed money and seen I was their way to get it.

I purchase an acre from her mother for $5,000.00 and the acre was worth $2,000.00.

I found out the daughter did not get a divorce and got an annulment. The family then turned against me because I would not stay with this lady. This isn't half of the story.

I live at 5813 Rover Drive just off 103rd Street. I am moving soon and I wanted this problem solved. I can sell that land and move in the Senior Citizen Home on Edgewood Ave.

The Attorneys want me to let go and not do anything but this is wrong and I am going to continue to fight.

Please any date pass the 18th would be fine.

I will make a donation when I sell that land.

Thanks again,

Ralph L. Watts

Subject: Re: My last request

To: ralphwatts@hotmail.com

From: dr.mac5@comcast.net

Date: Sun, 8 May 2011 17:02:35 +0000

I will check into this for you. Yes time is money and attorneys want to be paid in advance for their time. I would ask that you not pay me but make a monetary donation to my organization for my time. Are you willing to come to Jacksonville? I await your response. Sent via Blackberry from T-Mobile--------------------------
----

.

I been received a letter from the probate Judge and he said I can seek relief in Circuit Court. Every attorney seems afraid to go there and I think I know why.

On my last request if it becomes a reality I would like to have something like a bulletin board or one of those things that sits up and you flip paper over as you write. I need

To richard@goolsbylawfirm.com, Ralph Leon Watts

From: Ralph L. Watts (ralphwatts@comcast.net)

Sent: Sun 5/15/11 1:18 AM

To: richard@goolsbylawfirm.com

Cc: Ralph Leon Watts (ralphwatts@hotmail.com)

Hello,

I was told I need to get a Real Estate Attorney to resolve a probate case with an unusual ending.

This case is in Folkston, GA. I purchase an acre of land and cannot get the deed to the acre I purchase.

I visit other law firms and was told this was a sham case. I am not supposed to do anything to help myself. Because I am an old man (74) they feel like I cannot get help.

I need help and I would like to have the opportunity to present my case to you.

Please let me know if you can help. My phone is not a good one but I can get messages clear. 904-305-7224.

My email which I prefer is ralphwatts@hotmail.com.

Please let me hear from you.

Thanks,

Ralph Watts

Friday, July 01, 2011

Incident No. 11-0440

Statement to Police

On June 30, 2011 I received a call from Vivian Ingram. She told me my house has been burglarized and I should come immediately.

I was in Jacksonville, FL. I jumped in my car and drove for Folkston. When I reached Folkston I went to the Police Department and told them what had happen. I was told an Officer would meet me there.

I arrived there and the Officer arrives shortly. We look around the house to find my front screen was busted. At the rear of the house we notice the rear door was broken into. A vacuum cleaner and a BB rifle were left outside by the steps. Across the yard about 200 yards were some of my clothes.

218

Vivian Ingram is Kenneth Reed Jr. Aunt that called me and gave the investigating officer a statement.

From my house miss is just about everything. Some of the things right off I see missing were all my best clothes, CDs, two VCRs, ten VCR tapes two new crock pots two container of washing power. Some of these things were in a large locked trunk in my closet.

In my shed is what hurts. I have one large double locked trunk with new tools; they busted the locks off and took all. Inside the shed were two used and one new circular saw they took. It was more than $3500.00 of tools new an old in my shed.

I am making this report because it had to be more than one person stealing my things. They also had to have a large car to get all this stuff inside. Please I am begging you to catch these thieves.

If I am need for anything I can be contacted by the phone or email below.

The house now is not livable.

Thank you,

Ralph L. Watts

ON COUNTY SHERIFF OFFICE

RD STREET, SUITE C FOLKSTON, GA 31537

Incident Report

	Incident No.
	11-0440

	Counts	Code	Attem
RY(FORCED ENTRY-RESIDENCE)Felony	1	16-7-1 FE-RES	☐

cation			Secondary Location	
E HARVEY ROAD				
	State	Zip		County
ON	GA	31537		CHARLTON
Sub Zone		Location	Sub Location	Business Name

te	Time	Date	Time	Report Date	Time	Stranger	Weapon Type	Premise
1	11:00	To 06/30/2011	14:00	07/01/2011	16:36	No	HANDS / FIST, ETC	RESIDENCE
				Case Status				

nant

lame: (Last, First, Middle)					Work Phone
INGRAHAM VIVIAN					

n	Sex		Employer	School
	F			

Weight	Hair	Eyes	
	BLACK	BROWN	

Name: (Last, First, Middle)					Work Phone
WATTS RALPH					

IE HARVEY ROAD   FOLKSTON , GA 31537

	Sex		Employer	School
	M			

Weight	Hair	Eyes	

r

g Deputy	Badge	Suffix	Signature
Tommie A Spikes	2414		

ty Deputy	Badge	Suffix	Signature
Deputy Marty L Crews	2402		

220

Incident Report

	Model			Serial No

c CD's

nption	Property Type			
C.	**STOLEN PROPERTY**			
/alue		Jurd	Date	Location
$200.00		2	06/30/2011	
Value		Jurd	Date	Location
0.00				
Value		Other Description		

	Locker Location	
Not in property room		
	Seizing Officer	
	Voucher No.	

	Model			Serial No

wn

Players

tion	Property Type			
.	**STOLEN PROPERTY**			
Jue		Jurd	Date	Location
5.00		2	06/30/2011	
Jue		Jurd	Date	Location
.00				
Jue		Other Description		

	Locker Location	
t in property room		
	Seizing Officer	
	Voucher No.	

Race							
BLACK		M		Eyes	☐ Suspect	☐ Juvenile	☐ Wa
Height	Weight	Hair		BROWN	☐ Primary Aggressor		☑ Wa
6'00"	160	BLACK					

Court Name

Witness

Name: (Last, First, Middle)
INGRAHAM VIVIAN

Address
82 WILLIE HARVEY ROAD   FOLKSTON , GA 31537

Race	Sex		Employer	Schoo
BLACK	F			

Height	Weight	Hair	Eyes	
		BLACK	BROWN	

Property

Quantity	Make	Model	Serial No
1			

Description: **several mens clothes**

UCR Category Description	Property Type
CLOTHING, FURS	STOLEN PROPERTY

	Value	Jurd	Date	Location
☑ Stolen	$600.00	2	06/30/2011	
☐ Recovered	Value $0.00	Jurd	Date	Location
☐ Other	Value 0	Other Description		

☐ Evidence	Not in property room	Locker Location

Location Seized	Seizing Officer

Disposition	Voucher No

Reporting Deputy		Badge	Suffix	Signa
Officer Tommie A Spikes		2414		

Approving Deputy		Badge	Suffix	Signat
Chief Deputy Marty L Crews		2402		

222

1520 THIRD STREET, SUITE ...

Incident Report

Quantity	Make		Model	Serial No
2	unknown			

Description: crock pots

UCR Category Description	Property Type
MISCELLANEOUS	STOLEN PROPERTY

	Value	Jurd.	Date	Location
☑ Stolen	$100.00	2	06/30/2011	
☐ Recovered	$0.00	Jurd. Date		Location
☐ Other	0	Other Description		
☐ Evidence	Not in property room	Locker Location		

Location Seized | Seizing Officer

Disposition | Voucher No

Quantity	Make		Model	Serial No
1				

Description: various tools new and used

UCR Category Description	Property Type
MISCELLANEOUS	STOLEN PROPERTY

	Value	Jurd.	Date	Location
☑ Stolen	$3,500.00	2	06/30/2011	
☐ Recovered	$0.00	Jurd. Date		Location
☐ Other	0	Other Description		
☐ Evidence	Not in property room	Locker Location		

Location Seized | Seizing Officer

Disposition | Voucher No

Reporting Deputy | Badge Suffix

TON COUNTY SHERIFF OFFICE
00
HIRD STREET, SUITE C FOLKSTON, GA 31537

Incident Report

	Make	Model		Serial No
	unknown			

on: circular saws

tegory Description	Property Type			
LLANEOUS	**STOLEN PROPERTY**			

	Value	Jurd.	Date	Location
en	$120.00	2	06/30/2011	

	Value	Jurd.	Date	Location
overed	$0.00			

	Value	Other Description	
ther	0		

		Locker Location	
dence	Not in property room		

Seized		Seizing Officer	
on		Voucher No	

Entry ☐ Requested ☐ Warrant ☐ Missing Person ☐ Vehicle ☐ Article ☐
nal ☐A & B☐Supplemental☐Citation ☐ Accident ☐ Victim Bill of Rights ☐ Vehicl
nce Active

ve

en above times complainant states that she had seen Kenneth Reed Jr by F
ainant states that Reed told her he said he was getting his stuff from Watts
business there and needed to leave. Ingraham states she went to check th
ad been broken into. Ralph Watts came to check and noticed his shed was
ere are clothes and cookware missing from inside the house. Watts states t
aneous tools new and used stolen from the shed.

My house was torn and ram shacked. I could not live there if I wanted to. It was just like a tornado had struck my house.

You really don't know what a feeling you get from a situation like this unless it happens to you. You open a door and not only see your stuff missing but the house is torn apart.

Later I got news that the Sheriff had this guy in jail.

I sent him this letter.

Tuesday, August 23, 2011

Ralph L. Watts

P. O. Box 36

Folkston, GA 31537

Charlton County Sheriff Office

1520 Third Street, Suite C

Folkston, GA 31537

RE:Incident Number 11-0440

Dear Sir or Madam.

The first thing I want to say is "THANK YOU!!!!"

I came to your office yesterday (08-22-2011) and picked up this Incident Report.

I also learned that Kenneth Reed, Jr. was in custody. I am so thankful and grateful for you guys.

Kenneth Reed, Jr. burglarized my house, which I lost everything. My clothes which I had new jeans I never wore. He took suits, shirts, pants and all my personal items like different perfumes (never open) and toilet articles my children gave me for birthdays and holidays.

He took kitchen utilities, records & CDs, radios and office supplies. He even took two boxes of washing powder. My cabinet had locks, he broke all them. A trunk in my closet was double locked and he broke into it.

In my storage shed he took about $3,500.00 worth of tools. My storage had been double locked. He broke in and inside I had a large trunk that was double locked. He broke all the locks and left nothing that was saleable.

All this happen because Judge Philips made Robert Jordan Administrator of Elizabeth Jordan acre of land.

When Kenneth Reed burglarized my home, he trashed and scattered everything all over the floor.

226

Everything of value was taken. He vandalized my whole house. My bedroom, my computer room and my kitchen was burglarized. The back room where I hang all my clothes was also burglarized. He had to have a truck to haul all my things off.

That is the other reason I am writing this letter. He had to have an accomplice to do all what was done.

I was told it was his girl friend and I was also told it was his cousin. Kenneth Reed, Jr. had no car so he had to have help from someone.

Today I went to my house to scatter moth balls in every room. When my house was broken into the rear door was damaged. The bottom panel was missing and I know snakes came in. I want to run the snakes out before I try to clean up.

It will be awhile before I can stay there. If you want to know how it looked please ask Officer Spikes he seen this house condition.

I have not given a complete inventory listing of everything missing. This will not be until I can clean this mess up.

Once again I thank you all and after inventory I hope the Sheriff department will let me submit a final listing.

Very Thankful,

Ralph L. Watts

Monday, August 29, 2011Ralph L. Watts

P. O. Box 36

Folkston, GA 31537

Charlton County Sheriff Office

1520 Third Street, Suite C

Folkston, GA 31537

RE*: Incident Number 11-0440*

Sgt. King, I might have someone to visit Kenneth Reed, Jr. to help get some information from him.

I also found the serial number of one of my computers that was taken.It is a Pionex Computer, purchase from Phillip Jones (Navy)

266 MHz, 32mb 4GB Hard Drive; Serial # 5001858354.

1 Canon Printer IE: Multipass MP390 is missing: I have the installation CD

I also learned that a lady by the last name of Cobbs was his helper in this crime.

It supposes to be his girlfriend who drove the vehicle.

If she can be interrogated maybe she will give this guy up. If she can believe things will be better for her if she talks.

Also I want to tell you I received five (5) calls from 912-322-5486.

The first call was at 4:41pm, #2@11:05pm, #3@11:53pm, #4@11:54pm, #5@11:55pm.

All these calls were on 08-28-2011. They would not leave a message and when I tried to call no one would answer.

I believe who ever owns this number knows something.

Again I thank you all for a great job,

Ralph Watts

I have not heard anything about this case. I am the victim but I am an African American, poor and probably classified as nothing. I probably want hear anything because of that.

When I heard that Rose had got her son Kenneth Reed, Jr. out of jail I was really shocked. What in the world could she have told the sheriff to let him out? And to beat all she had the audacity to bring him out to where I live to audition to the family she is the boss.

Most men would pick up a gun and hurt all. That is too ugly for someone especially a mother to do. Bring the violator back to where the crime was committed and tell the world what he did is OK. This is not teaching children the right way to go. This makes children lawless and act very ugly like her child Kenneth Reed, Jr. does.

Back at Krystal in Jacksonville one of the Deacons made a remarkable explanation on my house burglary. He stated it's a possibility that Kenneth Reed, Jr. mother (Rose) knew you were here in Jacksonville and called her son in Folkston to rob your house.

I had to think about that because Rose was in a hurry to get him out of jail. Just think if my son done this to anyone I would want him in jail. I want him to learn this is not the thing to do to anyone.

I am the victim and would really like to know why and how she was able to get him out? Remember what she said about the deed; I can bet she told a good one to get her son out.

230

Why is all this information relevant? I want everyone to know what I had and having to deal with since 1994. The people I took to court in 2003 were very evil and had a mischievousness attitude. I always have taught love and was

fed stones. One family member mentions we are a family and we stick together.

When I heard this I had to laugh. Here I am helping Mr. Harvey pay taxes and this neighbor donates trouble with an ugly attitude.

To top things off they steps high with head in the air like they are important without an education. PLEASE!!!

If Kenneth Reed, Jr. would have burglarized the man that is living uptown he would still be in jail. Now he is out and probably break-in another African American home. This is so sad and that is the reason why I am writing this book.

I know certain people think because I am an old man I do not know how to get their ugly doings out. I will assure you I will continue and instructed my children to keep this going. We are not going to quit.

I want the whole world to know what happened here and why? What is probably happening in other towns?

I want this book printed in many languages and distributed over the world. I want the world to know what the real America is like.

231

We as Americans speak of uncivilized countries. America has a track record of doing, making and cultivating uncivilized activities.

235

236

Kenneth Reed Jr. just trashed my house. Every room was damaged and trashed.

Anyone does this to a person home have got a super problem.

This problem is soon going to show and someone will be in sorrow.

I have been working on my home now for six months. I am trying

to get all this trash out. I lost just about everything. Things I saved for fifty (50) years are gone.

When I look at cases like this I see where someone has been dogged out like me. They go mad and shoot everybody because they are hurt and no one cares. Someone somewhere has mistreated that person. We look at that person as crazy but we should look at why and who done it?

I have not heard anything about this case. I am the victim but I am an African American, poor and probably classified as nothing. I probably want hear anything because of that. Am I being fairly treated? NO!!!

This guy is supposed to be in jail without a bond. Why would they let Kenneth Reed Jr. out? This guy has an ugly track record.

Georgia Senior Citizen Source didn't give me any help. Florida Senior Citizen Source gave me good ideas on what to do to half way get going. I really thank them for helping me.

Let me add up some of the money I lost

Let's count up the money I lost. First my Attorney who did absolutely nothing charged me $3700.00. I paid Robert Jordan $5000.00 plus interest for the acre. I paid $500 to the Attorney in Atlanta, GA who did absolutely nothing, $90.00 to the Court Reporter which I was which I only owed half.

$5,000.00 to Willie and Lillie Mae Harvey.

What do I have now? I should have the deed to Elizabeth Jordan property but the Georgia Bar Association says attorneys can do their duty stuff and get by with it. (Like phony deeds)

I know this is happening but I still cannot grasp it. How do they think they can do something like this without someone finding out?

When I speak with other attorneys about this, some just shake their heads and walk off.. It should be some serious punishment behind this. Those that know better should not have done this. I paid for Elizabeth Jordan acre and it belongs to me.

I even tried to get help from the Georgia Senior Citizen Source and they refused to help me. I am 75 and I should be eligible for some assistance.

RE: Senior Help Request

1/30/12 Reply ▼Reply

 Jerrell Saddler Jerrell Saddlerjsaddler@scsatl.org

Send email

Find email Add to contactsTo ralphwatts@hotmail.com

From: Jerrell Saddler (jsaddler@scsatl.org)

Sent: Mon 1/30/12 7:09 AM

To: ralphwatts@hotmail.com

Attachments, pictures and links in this message have been blocked for your safety.

Show content | Always show content from jsaddler@scsatl.org

Mr. Watts,

I am not sure if Charlton County offers any assistance with Senior Home Repair, however; I am forwarding you their information to allow you to inquire. If I hear of any statewide programs I will be sure to forward the information your way.

Charlton County Senior Citizen Services

100 N 3rd Street

Folkston, GA 31537-3122

(912) 496-7372

Good Luck,

Jerrell L. Saddler

Director of Operations.

3/09/12 Reply ▼Reply

Hide details Diane Rogers Diane Rogersdrogers@concertedservices.org

240

Send email

Find email Add to contactsTo ralphwatts@hotmail.com

From: Diane Rogers (drogers@concertedservices.org)

Sent: Fri 3/09/12 9:16 AM

To: ralphwatts@hotmail.com

Attachments, pictures and links in this message have been blocked for your safety.

Show content | Always show content from drogers@concertedservices.org

Mr. Watts,

Natalie Dasher is our county coordinator in Charlton County. She is working on finding some resources for you. Unfortunately, there isn't any program that we're aware of that will do the type of work that you need, so she is having to do a lot of research to try and find a combination of resources. She has your contact information and will contact you next week. Thank you.

Diane C. Rogers

Community Services Director

Concerted Services, Inc.

(912) 557-6687 Reidsville Office

(912) 287-4088 Waycross Office

(912) 282-9123 Mobile

Sorry Diane Rogers, Natalie Dasher never contacted me.

Why do I have to go through all this?

My friends in Jacksonville get all kind of help from Florida Senior Source.

Why Georgia have to be different?

I even tried The Cochran Law Firm:

Thank you for contacting us!

4/03/12 Reply ▼Reply

The Cochran Firm The Cochran Firmwebintakes@cochranfirm.com

Send email

Find email Add to contactsTo Ralph Watts

From: The Cochran Firm (webintakes@cochranfirm.com)

Sent: Tue 4/03/12 1:57 PM

To: Ralph Watts (ralphwatts@hotmail.com)

Thank you very much for contacting Cochran Firm. Someone from our office will be contacting you shortly to address your questions and/or concerns. Again, we thank you for contacting us and look forward to speaking with you soon.

New|ReplyReply allForward|

I received this letter dated April 20, 2012 from The Cochran Firm.I think they thought I lived in Jacksonville, FLThey refused to help too. Well I have contacted numerous attorneys,

Law firms and people I thought could help.

I cannot get help; this is like the end.

Let me add up some of the money I lost Let's count up the money I lost. First my Attorney who did absolutely nothing charged me $3700.00. I paid Robert Jordan $5000.00 plus interest for the acre and did not get a deed. I paid $500 to the Attorney in Atlanta, GA who did absolutely nothing, $90.00 to the Court Reporter which I was only suppose to pay half ($45.00) plus other small items. All this together totals about $18,000.00 I lost because Judge Philips made Robert Jordan Administer of Elizabeth acre of land.

After paying Robert Jordan $5,000.00 I still do not have a deed for Elizabeth Jordan acre. Is this fair? Is this supposed to happen in a Court of Law? The attorneys got smart and refused to have an open court. Their court was in a back room closed to the public. The way crooks work; they put you in a squeeze where you cannot help yourself and no one else will. Therefore you lose; and that was the intention all alone. To take everything they can get legal or not.

Everyone will say he should have had an attorney. I had one and still he broke the law by charging me more than the law requires. He broke the law for not properly defending me. The firms that looked at this case state my attorney was helping the other guy.

The law states an attorney fee may not be more that 10 to 15 % of the value of the estate. This was an acre of land worth only $2000.00. I was charged $3700.00. How can you fix a mouth to say this is law or try to anything to defend these actions.

I explain this to the Georgia's Bar Association. I filed a grievance (Bar#491500) with the Grievance Counsel. (Copy enclosed) According to the letter received from Carmen Rojas Rafter more information is needed.

They finally agreed with the attorney. Can someone be so ugly and out there they do a thing like this. It is awful; they did not investigate like they said. No one came and spoke to me. If they would have investigated this would not come out the way it did, this is very serious. These attorneys swindle me out of my money. I cannot believe this or the Courts let them get away with this.

Now if I was one of those guys living uptown I would not have this trouble.

If Kenneth Reed Jr. broke in their house and stole and tore it up I am sure he would still be in Jail. Most of all they would have investigated to find and would find out who had and purchase their items.

If one of those guys living up town filed a report like this there would have been some serious investigations.

That is what I get for moving here; I had no idea ugly things still exist in this age. People like this should not be a supervisor's or hold a responsible position.

I also filed a fee complaint with the Georgia Bar Association. According to Rita Payne, Fee Arbitration Director they agreed with the attorney. What the law says dose not matter when it comes to an old poor African American.

This is totaling ashamed that we have to endure this type of treatment from ones who we trust to protect us.

If I were wealthy these types of things do not happen. When you are poor and an African American no one cares. This hurt because I believe there are many cases where these types of treatment exist.

I listen to Joel Osteen at Lakewood Church in Houston, Texas. His inspirations help me to keep going hoping that someday an honest law abiding Attorney or Judge would get involve and straight this out in a real Court of Law not in a back room.. The law should be strict and perjury should not be ignored.

The one thing I want all to know; My Father in Heaven will help me. You might not tell me or anyone else but in your lifetime you will regret what you did to me. You will see the ugliness surrounding this case from the development to the end. All your friends will read this book of your involvement. How you helped or stood by without helping with the law.

When a person hears about someone they know have cancer or met a violent death. There are reasons why these things occur. Who can say they do not know it reason but, I will say somewhere in this person's life lives a dark side.

I find no joy in these sayings because it is written "Whosoever believeth in me shall have everlasting life" We all are entitle to everlasting life. In order for this to happen we must have a true life here on earth.

Now I sit here on land I paid for twice. No deed to prove its mine. My old house was trash and heavily damaged. No deed and the Courts know what happen but refuse to help.

I needed some help so I call the Georgia Senior Source. I did hear from them so I called a local business here in Folkston.

When I call the business in Folkston I spoke with Bo Todd's son or nephew. He said he was some kin to Bo Todd. Never-the-less he gave me Bo Todd number.

I called Bo Todd and told him my problem, I told him where I live and before I could finish speaking with him he hung up. I was in Jacksonville, FL.

When I got to Folkston one neighbor told me some men were waiting on me. Bo Todd had sent some men right out soon as he hung up. So now I had to call Bo Todd.

I called Bo Todd and was really surprised. He expressed how angry he was for me not being at home. He was furious and I just listen until he stopped.

When he stopped I apologized for not being at home. I also told him I do not want his help. If I got to listen to ugly talk when I am in distress; it will kill me. So I flatly told him I do not want his help.

I thought Bo Todd was a Christian. On the phone he sounds like anything but a Christian. Then it came to me that Rose had gone to get her son out and probably used Bo Todd help and said some ugly things about me. This is what I think what happen. Even if Rose told him ugly things about me I think he should have conducted himself in a professional way. I say this because Rose's mother Lillie Mae Harvey is a good friend of Bo Todd. In this case Rose probably said things about me to Bo Todd so she can get help to get her son out of jail. (This is what I think)

I called Florida Senior Source to see if they could help me.

The guy told me he could not come but told me everything I needs to do to get my water running, closing up my back door and how to keep my lights from going out. I have great respect for this propitious young man. Georgia needs a few of these.

250

Thank God for Florida Senior Source. Georgia needs to wake up.

My house may never get repaired. When Kenneth Reed Jr. burglarized and trashed and he also stopped up my bathroom sink and turned the hot water on. The hot water just kept running until the heater burned out. That is too terrible a thing to do.

When the Police and I arrived we did not get to the back because of the trashing he done. We did not know the water was running. The hot water just ran, ran and ran. Many pieces of tile from the wall fell down because of the heat from the hot water.

How did I find out? I received a large light bill and called the light company..

I told them the only thing could possibly be running is my refrigerator, why is my light bill so high?

The lady looked at the monitor and said no-no there is something running right now at your house.

I jumped in my car and came to Folkston. I jumps over all the trash in the living room and trashed in the bedroom to get to the light junction box. I pulled out the fuse box and cut everything off.

It hurt so bad I stayed away for a couple of months. I could not bear to see my house mess up so badly. My pressure went to the roof. My insurance told me they cannot cover me out of my area. I went without High Blood Pressure for six (6) months.

I got a friend to help me start clean up most of the stuff. It took us a month to get to the back of the house. When we got to the back of the house we really found a mess. This was a terrible sight. Everything in the back was destroyed.

The hot water from the bathroom made the wall tiles weak, loose and falling down. The bathroom door will not close. The bathroom sink and cabinet destroyed. My bathroom was unusable.

In the kitchen all the underneath of the sink was ruined. This whole thing was just a mess.

It is so sad to know of anyone that could do this. Things were so bad that everything in the back room had to be thrown away.

Rose's son Kenneth, Jr. was always bad. Remember the letter I wrote to Rose about her son in 2003. He is a bad and trifling kid and somewhere down the line a life is going to be lost because of him.

He has done enough to go to prison for a long time. If not and something happens or someone get hurt the law enforcement will be responsible.

So I sit here; paid for an acre of land I cannot get, my house burglarized and trashed and law enforcement turns the guy loose. I have lost all my money because two attorneys swindled me. They

probably would say you signed the papers to what happen but it was a con. It a swindle and I will say this to the end. Whenever you do something to someone without their knowledge and you know it wrong; it's a scam.

My whole mind just seems to go and come. My mind is really assassinated.

What in the world am I going to do?

I can see years off my life because Robert Jordan was given authority he was not entitle to. When the mortgage companies mortgaged the land; why didn't they go through Probate Court? They got part of the land like I did.

Should've the Probate Judge notice this? This is a Probate Court and all the tricks a Probate Judge should know. Whenever something looks strange he should investigate before making a decision.

At the Probate Court meeting I drew lines as to how the property was laid out. I showed the Judge the lines for Elizabeth Jordan acre and the lines Lillie Mae Harvey deeded to me. This should have thrown up a red flag. I presented enough evidence to warrant an investigation.

]An investigation would have proved that I was correct but I was not given the chance. I did not have an attorney present therefore he just went alone with the attorney present.

The way things seem as I can get up and speak the truth and it's not credible.

It has to come from an attorney. This is very sad to have this type of setup.

This is because I am a poor old African American and was used by two (2) attorneys and Robert Jordan. If this is not a swindle, there isn't one anywhere.

No matter what I will continue this story everywhere. I intend to let this be known not only in the United States but other countries as well.

We speak about people in other countries and how uncivilized they are. What right we have to speak when we treat our own people in an uncivilized way. What do we have? "3647" going around taking people money by using the Court system. They are not Honorable at all; they are "3647".

We suppose to have Honorable people serving in our Court system.

They knew this is wrong. What also hurts is there are lawyers and Judges heard this story and refuse to say anything or lend a hand. Honorable people do not turn their backs to ugly problems and situations.

It would not hurt so badly if I would have got what I paid for. I paid for Elizabeth Jordan acre of land. Those ugly people want to push a phony deed off on me. The deed is phony because it is not the right one.

And you know they don't care; they feel like I cannot do anything about it and I have to take the ugliness they presents. They never were so wrong in their whole life. I have not got warm up yet. Every publication will have something about this case. You are going to be in the news and chat-rooms.

Judge Phillips gave Robert Jordan Administrator of Elizabeth Jordan acre only. His attorney comes giving me a deed of property that belongs to Lillie Mae Harvey. That is very, very crazy.

Remember that attorney Churchill who I sent $500.00 to write a letter. It took three months to even get a conversation after threats were made. I want you to read the letter he sent to me itemizing why I owe him that money. Remember the money was sent to have a letter written:

256

you want your letter to state changed from when we last spoke on November 26, 2010.
However, I cannot honor your request to fully refund your retainer. That would not be a
fair solution. We should be able to work this out. I look forward to hearing from you on
this matter.

Yours truly,

WILLIAM P. CHURCHILL, III, PC

William P. Churchill III
Attorney At Law

W/Enclosure

Cc   File

Mr. Ralph Watts
P. O. Box 9464
Jacksonville, FL 32208

10-1033-001:

Professional Fees

Date		Description	Hours	Rate
9/3/2010	WPC	File Review.	1.00	250.00
10/28/2010	WPC	Voice Mail. Telephone call to number found on Google beleived to be that of client. Left message on voice mail to call back.	0.02	250.00
11/14/2010	WPC	Email Exchange. Received message from client.	0.02	250.00
11/15/2010	WPC	Document review. E-mail reviewed.	0.02	250.00
11/15/2010	WPC	Email Exchange. Sent reply to client.	0.15	250.00
11/24/2010	WPC	Telephone Call - Outgoing. Telephone call to client. Mr. Jordan, father of Lillie Mae's father died and left property to her. Approxamately 13 acres. She took one-half of acre and deeded it to mortgage company to pay for her father's funeral expenses. She sold client other half. He has deed. Her brother Robert said that's his mother's land and client can't have it. Court awarded him executor over her estate of the one-acre. Attorneys told him Lillie Mae had no right to sell one-half acre to client. He paid her $7k. He wants quit claim deed to entire acre of land, or money back. Told him could possibly get $7k he paid to Lillie Mae, plus $5k he paid to Robert, plus attorneys fees and costs. He said hold off sending letter until we talk again. Asked him to send copy of proof of payment for land to Lillie Mae and Robert.	0.45	250.00
11/29/2010	WPC	Correspondence received from client. Received and reviewed letter from client.	0.10	250.00
12/24/2010	WPC	Voice Mail. Telephone call from client. Left message on voice mail to call back re status.	0.05	250.00
1/21/2011	WPC	Correspondence received from client. Demanded all work stop, and return initial retainer of 500.00.	0.10	250.00
2/21/2011	WPC	Correspondence received from client.	0.10	250.00
3/4/2011	WPC	Document preparation. Letter to client.	0.50	250.00

Sub-total Fees:
Discount: Flat Fee reached

Rate Summary

William P. Churchill   2.50 hours at $250.00/hr   623.75

258

Total hours: 2.50

Payments

3/4/2011	Payment	Trust application	500.00
		Sub-total Payments	500.00

Trust Account

			Beginning Balance:	0.00
6/24/2010				500.00
3/4/2011	Trust application			-500.00
			Ending Balance	0.00

Total Current Billing:	500.00
Previous Balance Due:	0.00
Total Now Due:	0.00

Pretty good HUH? I wonder do they teach that stuff in law school. This guy sits down and make up some false charges in order to keep my money.

259

I sent that money for a letter to be written. I must say that again, the $500.00 was sent to have a letter written. The letter was not written and you are not supposed to keep the money. This is really too facetious for anyone in their right mind to do.

Some might read this and laugh about it; but it is sick. Why would you take someone money they trusted you to do a job and you decide you going to do something else? Will they say you are an intelligent human being? NO!!!!

I also asked McGee and Churchill to send my materials to me. You think somewhere along the line they would do something right. They did not.

What kind of attorneys these men are? They know the law but it's because they know who I am; an old African American with retirement money taken by slick dealing attorneys. These are great attorneys if you listen to the Bar Association. Why would they call themselves Americans?

This is one thing I want people to know about the Georgia Bar Association.

They know they should have done something in my case. They refused to take time for an old African American who has been treated unfairly. We (Bar) cannot lose time on someone one is not important to us. That is what it amount to; an old poor African American cannot waste our time.

This is the Law:

If you've fired your lawyer, he's required to give a copy of the file he created for your case to the new lawyer (or to you,

if you're representing yourself). **It's illegal for an attorney to hold the file hostage, even if you owe him money**.

What is the matter with the Bar? Can someone there read the law? Or it does not matter.

There is no use in me contacting the Georgia Bar Association. That is a waste of time because no matter they are going to agree with the attorney.

Their actions tell me they do not know the law or because I am a Senior African American and they do not care.

I am sure The Florida Bar Association and many other states Bar Association would not tolerate this type of actions from their attorneys. Their attorneys have great respect for the law and themselves.

One Georgia attorney personally told me to hurry and file memo against this case. If I wait too long the Courts cannot do anything.

I just looked at him; if the Courts let someone becomes Administrator after twenty (20) years of loans and mortgages on a piece of divided land. Afterward they find out there have been some wrong doing with this case in about a couple of years; and they cannot do something? Please do not tell me this. It's amazing what some people will say to defend an unlawful action.

These unlawful actions terrified involved persons. The results for any wrongdoing should be liable for restitutions.

I cannot get an attorney because I do not have the money. I cannot get my house fixed because I do not have any money and Georgia Senior Source will not help. I have to ask for outside help.

I have lost about $18,000.00 in this case.

Over $8,500.00 was taken from my home.

To fix this house back is about $4,700.00

To pay an Attorney $???????? Who knows?

Do you see what I am facing? Just because Robert Jordan was made Administrator of something he shouldn't have. If Elizabeth Jordan acre was probate able it should have been twenty (20) years ago when Lillie Mae Harvey first mortgage a part of the acre. Doesn't that make sense? Please everyone should not act dumb or crazy; this is wrong.

Mortgage companies didn't go through Probate so why should I? An excellent question; who would like to respond to that one?

Mortgage companies have a piece of Elizabeth Jordan acre like I have.

This is just plain wrong, wrong. There is no room for anyone to makeup a lie to make it right.

I can visualize someone trying to say this was a mistake. Belonia!! I wrote Robert Jordan attorney and ask him to please make sure my

deed read exactly like the one Joe Jordan issued to Elizabeth Jordan. He issued one like Lillie Mae Harvey which they said was wrong. Now, they are doing worst than that; issuing a phony deed to me. Robert Jordan does not have the right to give me a deed for Lillie Mae Harvey private land.

I will say this; anyone who would do something like this is very, very low.

Your mind is gone to even think this is right.

Right now I just want to get my right mind back. The worrying and harassing I received is torture. They have destroyed most of my mind.

Not only my mind assassinated, I feel like I have been buried alive.

I hear often that the guy (Kenneth Reed, Jr.) always comes to the house across the street. It is very hard to see the man that destroyed my home, stole things I saved for fifty (50) years and riding around having fun like nothing happen. But this is Folkston, Georgia and there are difference laws here.

There just is no Law and Order here for Senior African Americans. If the man uptown house was destroyed; Kenneth Reed, Jr. would still be in jail. This is very hard living like this. I do not feel well; I do not wish to speak in person or on the phone with anyone. I just cannot handle it.

If there is an attorney who wish to help or anyone who wishes to provide some answers please send to address below. Right now I do not wish to see anyone in person. I have been assassinated and

My livelihood buried.

A complaint will be filed about this everywhere I can.

I will continue tell newspapers, TV personalities, etc. I will not quit.

This is too ugly.

Honorable Judge Jackson should have had this case investigated. He should have made them come before him and explain this case.

Judge Jackson passed before completing this book. I always wanted to personally thank him for sending my case before a Jury. He thought something was wrong here and the Jury would be the best for results.

Those slick attorneys knew this was not a good move for them. They had their backroom court. Isn't this ugly?

My attorney told the Georgia Bar that this case was settled in an open court. He lied; this was settled in a backroom.

Why wouldn't they investigate? I gave enough evidence that there were problems.

All these people should go to jail for this.

Thank you,

Ralph L. Watts

Copyright 2012

ISBN No. 978-0-9858029-5-0